A Yankee Spy in Richmond

A YANKEE SPY IN RICHMOND

The Civil War Diary of "Crazy Bet" Van Lew

edited by
David D. Ryan

STACKPOLE
BOOKS

Published by
STACKPOLE BOOKS
5067 Ritter Road
Mechanicsburg, PA 17055

Printed in the United States of America

10 9 8 7 6 5 4 3 2 1

First edition

Materials from the Elizabeth Van Lew Papers, Rare Books and Manuscripts
Division, New York Public Library, Astor, Lenox, and Tilden Foundations are
used with permission.

Library of Congress Cataloging-in-Publication Data

Van Lew, Elizabeth L., 1818–1900.
    A Yankee spy in Richmond : the Civil War diary of "Crazy Bet" Van
Lew / edited by David D. Ryan.
        p.   cm.
    Includes bibliographical references (p.).
    ISBN 0-8117-0554-4
    1. Van Lew, Elizabeth L., 1818–1900—Diaries. 2. United States—
History—Civil War, 1861–1865—Secret service. 3. Spies—Virginia—
Richmond—Diaries. 4. Women spies—Virginia—Richmond—Diaries.
5. Richmond (Va.)—History. I. Ryan, David D. II. Title.
E608.V34A3   1996
973.7'85—dc20   96-10623
                                                                CIP

To
The Reverend Robin Christopher Ryan, C.P.

CONTENTS

FOREWORD

As a Richmond native, I have always been fascinated with the stories of Elizabeth Van Lew, the nineteenth-century woman who lived in the mansion on the city's Church Hill. She was General Ulysses S. Grant's spy in Richmond during the Civil War. As her deeds became known during and after the war, she was ostracized by Richmond society. Five years ago I began collecting copies of her papers, letters, and "Occasional Journal" in an attempt to bring them together from their various archives and to tell her story.

Aiding me in my effort were the John Stewart Bryan Memorial Foundation and D. Tennant Bryan, my former boss at Richmond Newspapers for nearly twenty-one years. I wish also to thank my editor, William C. Davis, and the publisher, Stackpole Books. Wayne Furman, Office of Special Collections, New York Public Library, aided me with the Van Lew papers, including the original copy of the "Occasional Journal" and letters. I am grateful to Mr. Furman and the New York Public Library for allowing me to use the Van Lew papers in their collection. John M. Coski, historian at the Museum of the Confederacy, gave me valuable aid, as did Conley Edwards and other staff members of the Virginia State Library and Archives; Kathleen Albers at the Richmond Newspapers Library; Francis Pollard and associates at the Virginia Historical Society; Margaret Cook of the Swem Library of the College of William and Mary; Arthur B. House of the National Archives; William S. Simpson, Jr., of the Richmond Public Library; Robert W. Waitt, grandson of Thomas McNiven; and the staff of the Valentine Museum, Richmond.

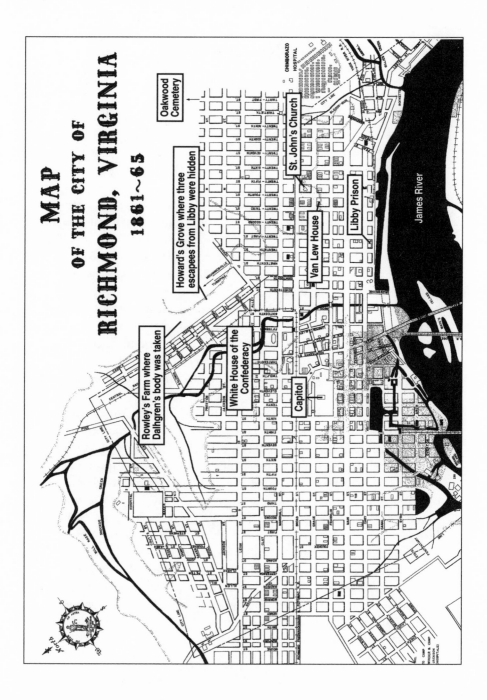

MAP
OF THE CITY OF
RICHMOND, VIRGINIA
1861~65

Oakwood Cemetery

Howard's Grove where three escapees from Libby were hidden

St. John's Church

Van Lew House

Libby Prison

James River

Rowley's Farm where Dalhgren's body was taken

White House of the Confederacy

Capitol

CHIMBORAZO HOSPITAL

INTRODUCTION

All wars produce spies, and the Civil War was no exception. There were those spies who provided information for only one reason—money—and there were those who provided information out of a sense of duty to a cause. A slave told where Confederate units were located; a white merchant told a Confederate general of movements of Federal cavalry. Most spies have gone unrecognized throughout history, but others have become famous and their stories have been recounted in books. The Civil War had both kinds, for there were literally thousands of them on both sides.

Some of the most famous spies of the Civil War included women. Rose Greenlaw and Belle Boyd are two examples. Mrs. Greenlaw, a Washington socialite, provided Confederate General P. G. T. Beauregard with information on Federal troop movements toward Bull Run in 1861. For nine more months she sent information to the Confederates that she gained through her social contacts. Finally in April 1862 she was made to move to Virginia by the Federals to prevent her from gaining access to more information. Boyd, a seventeen-year-old girl, provided General Thomas "Stonewall" Jackson with information on Federal troops during Jackson's 1862 Shenandoah Valley campaign. She was arrested twice and in 1863 moved to England to escape being arrested again. Timothy Webster of Perrymansville, Maryland, spied for the private agency of Allan Pinkerton. Webster made many forays into Virginia to retrieve information valuable to the Union, but he was captured by Confederate detectives in Richmond. On April 29, 1862, he became the first spy of the Rebellion to be hanged. His sweetheart, Hattie Lewis, was imprisoned in Richmond's Castle Thunder for a year.

By the winter of 1862–63, General John Henry Winder, Henrico District provost marshal, had his hands full trying to control the loyalist spies in Richmond. Among those his detectives arrested was former Virginia Congressman John Minor Botts. A loyalist, Botts was confined for several weeks in Castle Godwin and then placed under house arrest for suspicion of spying. He was never tried.[1]

Another suspected Federal spy watched by General Winder was William Alvan Lloyd, a New York and Baltimore businessman. A well-known publisher of railroad and steamboat guides and maps of the South, Lloyd used his business to travel throughout the South to collect information as President Abraham Lincoln's personal spy. To get in Winder's good graces, he bought the general a $1,200 custom-made uniform as well as other gifts. But Winder had his suspicions and ordered Lloyd watched. Lloyd, however, was still able to provide Lincoln with information and maps of Confederate ports and of troop movements, even being so brash as to live for a time in the Virginia cities of Lynchburg and Danville.[2]

On the other side, Jerome Clarke, a hard-fighting guerrilla in the western theater, used his feminine looks to dress up as a flirtatious woman and spy on the Federals. This "woman" was known as "Sue Mundy."[3]

Perhaps one of the most interesting spies was a Richmond native. She did not spy for her state, but rather for the Union. And even though she was under the constant threat of being discovered, she kept a secret diary about her efforts. Had her diary been found during the war, she surely would have been tried as a spy and probably hanged. While portions of her "Occasional Journal" have been quoted in previous books, the entire existing journal and her letters have never been brought together and edited until now. This is her journal, her letters, her story.

John Van Lew, prominent Richmond businessman, friend of U.S. Chief Justice John Marshall, and owner of black servants, died September 14, 1843. His funeral service, conducted at his Richmond, Virginia, Church Hill mansion, was attended by hundreds of friends from Richmond, New York, and Philadelphia. Fifty-seven years later his daughter, Elizabeth, died in the same mansion. She was buried at the family plot in Shocke Hill Cemetery, but her grave went unmarked. Years later some friends from Massachusetts sent a granite stone to mark the site, but as far as most Richmonders were concerned, the spot could have gone unmarked forever. The plaque placed on the stone told why:

ELIZABETH VAN LEW

1818–1900

She risked everything that is dear to man—friends, fortune, comfort, health, life itself, all for one absorbing desire of her heart—that slavery might be abolished and the Union preserved.

Elizabeth Louisa Van Lew, code name "Babcock," was a spy for the Union, sending military and other information to Generals George H. Sharpe, chief of the U.S. Bureau of Military Information (Secret Service); Benjamin F. Butler, commander of the Army of the James; George G. Meade, commander of the Army of the Potomac; and Ulysses S. Grant, overall commander of Union forces during the last year of the war. She also provided Union soldiers in Richmond prisons with bribe money, food, and books; hid escaped prisoners in her home and at friends' homes; and instigated the Kilpatrick-Dahlgren raid on Richmond in 1864 to free Union prisoners. She spent all of her inheritance buying and freeing slaves and pursuing her anti-Confederacy efforts.

Elizabeth wrote of her work as a spy in her "Occasional Journal" but was constantly in fear that it and the work she was doing for the Union military would be discovered. "The keeping of a complete journal was a risk too fearful to run. Written only to be burnt was the fate of almost everything which would now be of value."[4]

Fortunately she did not burn the journal, but she did bury it for some time. Her fears of recrimination from Southerners continued after the war, and on December 16, 1866, she went to the U.S. War Department and requested that every message she sent during the conflict be returned to her. All were returned, except a few that had been overlooked, and she destroyed the notes.[5]

Elizabeth was born October 15, 1818, in Richmond, the first of three children of John and Eliza Louise Baker Van Lew. The Van Lew (Van Lewen) family immigrated to America in 1660.[6] Her father was born March 4, 1790, in Jamaica, Long Island. Her mother, born in Philadelphia in 1798, was the daughter of Hilary Baker, a former mayor of the friendship city. John and Eliza met in Richmond and were married at St. John's Church on January 10, 1818. Their other children were Anna Paulina, born October 7, 1820, and John Newton, born August 26, 1823. The family's first home was located on the south side of I Street (later Marshall Street) between Twenty-fourth and Twenty-fifth Streets. In 1836 John purchased a three-story mansion in the 2300 block of East Grace Street on Church Hill. He bought the house from John Adams, physician, developer, and mayor of the city from 1819 to 1825.[7] Built of stucco walls, the large home was trimmed in Scotch limestone, brought over as ballast in pre-Revolutionary ships. Twin semicircular steps with iron balusters led up on either side of the stone front porch. An eighteen-foot-wide hall extended from the front to the rear of the house, where a splendid piazza gave the Van Lews a commanding view of the James River to the south and the city to the west and north.[8]

John Van Lew had moved to Richmond because of an unspecified illness, probably a respiratory ailment, that grew worse over the years. Nevertheless, he was able to establish a successful merchandising business, owning five hardware stores. He doted on his children. "I remember my father coming in at night and waking and taking us up in our long white flannel gowns to sit awhile on his knee, to be pressed to his heart," recalled Elizabeth. "My parents were both intellectual and devoted to books. Fifty dollars a year was allowed to buy books."[9] The Van Lew house became the center of social gatherings. Among the guests were the Marshalls and the Richmond families of the Lees, the Robinsons, the Wickhams, the Adamses, the Cabels, and the Carringtons. Edgar Allan Poe once read his poem "The Raven" in the Van Lew parlor. The family rode through the city in a carriage pulled by six white horses, and they would often travel to White Sulphur and Sweet Springs in the western mountains of Virginia for vacation and to restore John's health. In the earliest existing family letter, Mrs. Van Lew wrote her cousin, Charles J. Richards, on April 2, 1838, from Sweet Springs, telling him she was learning to swim and the latest news of who was at the resort.[10]

Two years later, Mr. Van Lew wrote Richards from Philadelphia, mentioning his illness. "As regards my health, I hardly know what to say. My life at best some year past has been but . . . 'miserable,' one day better and the next worse. Two days ago I was laid out. . . . I am again confined to the house."[11] Three years later, when Elizabeth was twenty-five, he died "after a severe and protracted illness."[12]

John Van Lew left the house and his other real estate to his wife, and a $10,000 endowment to each of his children.[13] Part of the property consisted of a parcel of land across the street. Upon it Mrs. Van Lew built two houses, which she rented out for additional income.[14]

As a child in the early 1830s, Elizabeth had been sent to Philadelphia for school. While there she was under the influence of a governess who spoke strongly for the abolition of slavery. This influence and a girl she met at the springs probably formed Miss Van Lew's own abolitionist feelings. John Albee, a Boston researcher who spent twenty years around the turn of the century studying Elizabeth Van Lew, said, "I have repeatedly asked those who knew Miss Van Lew for some explanation of her activities on behalf of the slave, though she owned slaves herself." In his notes at the Swem Library of the College of William and Mary, he recorded that one of Elizabeth's friends recalled Miss Van Lew saying that as a girl she had gone to Hot Springs and there met a daughter of a slave trader.

"This girl told Miss Van Lew that once her father had for sale a slave mother and her young babe, and that when the mother found that she had been sold to one purchaser and parted from her babe, who had been sold to another, the mother's heart broke and she fell dead. Miss Van Lew said that she never forgot that fearful story and its effect lasted for her life."[15] Soon after the death of her father, she convinced her mother to free their nine slaves, and Elizabeth used some of the money generated by her endowment to purchase relatives of the servants and to free them.

Writer Fredrika Bremer, a native of Finland, visited Richmond in 1854. She recalls meeting Elizabeth:

June 18th. I have, both yesterday and to-day, received a great number of . . . invitations. [One of them] was [from] a Mrs. Van L., a widow and her daughter; intellect, kindness and refinement of feeling were evident in their gentle countenances. The daughter, a pleasing, pale blonde, expressed so much compassion for the sufferings of the slave, that I was immediately attracted to her. She drove me out yesterday to see the lovely environs of Richmond. . . . We . . . drove to a large tobacco manufactory. . . . Here I heard the slaves, about a hundred in number, singing at their work in large rooms; they sung quartettes, choruses, and anthems, and that so purely, and in such perfect harmony, and with such exquisite feeling, that it was difficult to believe them self-taught. . . . Good Miss Van L. could not refrain from weeping.[16]

Miss Bremer was invited to the home of a slave owner, but after seeing the slaves at the warehouse, she refused the invitation.[17]

Elizabeth was one of the belles of Richmond and considered pretty in her youth, but she never married. Albee speculated Miss Van Lew may have been involved in a failed romance that left her forever bitter.

While Elizabeth's brother, John Newton, following in his

father's footsteps, operated a successful hardware business, she and her mother continued their frequent trips to the springs. Writing her son from White Sulphur Springs in 1860, Eliza Van Lew noted, "Your sister and myself like these Springs better than any we've ever been. The air and water agree with us. They have very good bread, tea and coffee. . . . E. and I walk a great deal . . . to the top of the mountain, over the tunnel."[18]

But their carefree lives were soon to change. As word spread through Richmond society of the Van Lews' antislavery feelings, social invitations stopped coming. Elizabeth's determination to fight against slavery solidified shortly after her forty-first birthday in 1859, when she learned of John Brown's raid on Harpers Ferry, his subsequent capture by Colonel Robert E. Lee, and his hanging.

"I have always thought him one who suffered so deeply with the slaves," she wrote in one of the first pages of her journal.[19] From that time on, she added, Southern people were in a "palpable state of war. They thirsted for it; they cried out for it. It was not enough that one old man should die. No plea of people . . . would be listened to."[20] She determined she would do all in her power to see the South defeated, the slaves freed, and the Union reunited. Richmond's population was composed of large numbers of Scots, Huguenot French, Germans, Portuguese, and Jews, many of whom were loyalists. Elizabeth called on her loyalist neighbors in Church Hill for help with her dangerous plan to give information to Unionists.

"Mobs went to private houses to hang the true of heart," Elizabeth wrote. "Loyalty now was called treason, and cursed. If you spoke in your parlor or chamber, to your next of heart, you whispered."[21]

Despite threats from local Confederates, Elizabeth went on with her plans. The Van Lews owned a small vegetable farm near the Richmond-Henrico County line, abutting the James River and the Osborne Turnpike. She used it from the beginning of the war as the first of five points along the James River to pass along information to the Federal forces at Fortress Monroe in Hampton.

The farm also was the first relay point for intelligence she sent in 1864 and 1865 to General Grant at City Point near Petersburg.[22] Information was delivered by servants carrying baskets of eggs. One egg in each basket was hollow and contained her notes, which she had torn into small pieces. In addition, notes were carried in the soles of the servants' shoes. She devised her own code consisting of a series of numbers and letters. By placing coded notes into the spines of books, she used the cipher to get information into and out of the prisons, particularly Libby Prison, where most of the captured Union officers were held.

The first real test of Elizabeth's ability to intercommunicate with the prisoners came in July 1861, when more than 600 Union prisoners were brought to Richmond after the July 21 First Battle of Bull Run. Among those captured was New York Congressman Alfred Ely, who had left Washington to watch what was thought would be the defeat of the Confederacy. In the rout of the Yankees Ely was caught up with fleeing Union soldiers. They hid in the woods at Bull Run and were captured at the same time. The prisoners arrived on July 24 and were crammed into Legion's Warehouse and Tobacco Factory at the corner of Main and Twenty-fifth Streets. The following day the officers were separated from the enlisted men and placed in the adjoining Harwood's Warehouse, which General Winder had commandeered.

Elizabeth soon made contact with the Union officers at Harwood, taking them books and food. But her contact with the prisoners, and particularly her aid and comfort of the injured, soon brought public criticism. Although not naming the Van Lews, an article in the July 31, 1861, *Richmond Enquirer* clearly referred to them and condemned their activities.[23]

But Elizabeth was too feisty and determined to let the criticism stop her, and she put herself in precarious situations time after time. Toward the end of 1861, she learned that Congressman Ely's civilian friend Calvin Huson of Rochester was seriously ill and dying at Harwood Prison, where he too was held prisoner after being captured at the First Battle of Bull Run. She and her mother, a more cautious loyalist, offered to attend to him at their home, and the Confederate officials finally agreed. "They [the Confederate prison officials] had procured for him a boarding-place in the family of Mrs. John Van Lew, a wealthy person, living in one of the finest mansions in Richmond," wrote Ely in his diary October 9, 1861. "This evening Mr. [Jackson] Warner [prison commissary] reported to me that he had just come from Mrs. Van Lew's, and that Mr. Huson was better, and had remarked that he would give one hundred dollars if his family could see for one moment how comfortably situated he was, and the care the ladies took of him," Ely added two days later.[24] In a reference on October 14, Ely told of meeting Elizabeth at Harwood Prison. "I at once recognized [her] as the same lady who had visited our quarters on the second day after my arrival."[25] Mr. Huson died October 14, and the Van Lews buried him in their family plot at Shockoe Hill Cemetery.

In early 1862 Miss Van Lew received notice that Confederate Chief Surgeon Edward G. Higgenbotham had decided she could no longer bring food to sick Union prisoners. Instead of defeating her efforts, the notice increased her resolve. Carrying some custard she was planning to take to the sick prisoners, she and two unnamed lady friends charged into the office of Assistant Secretary of War A. G. Bledsoe and demanded that the order be rescinded. Bledsoe was sympathetic and promised to refer her request to Secretary of War Judah P. Benjamin. Bledsoe kept the custard and ate it after the ladies left. Benjamin referred her request to General Winder, who said he would not interfere, but who later restored her privileges.

In January 1862 Paul Joseph Revere, the great-grandson of the Revolutionary Paul Revere, was one of eight Union prisoners removed from Harwood Prison and put in a small cell in the Henrico County Jail. They were selected to be held as hostages for Confederate privateers who had been captured aboard the *Savannah* at New York and were being threatened with hanging as pirates. Elizabeth immediately went to the jail, taking the prisoners food and books, and befriending Revere. "A lady, Miss Van Lew, has been allowed to send us some books, which were very acceptable, as our stock was quite limited," Revere wrote his family from his jail cell on January 10. "A lady of this place has sent us, on several occasions, various nice things," he added in another letter six days later.[26] The hostages were exchanged the following month. Revere was killed during the Battle of Gettysburg, but his family would not forget Miss Van Lew's kindness to him.

Libby Warehouse was commandeered by Winder on March 26, 1862, to be used as the city's main prison. It became home to most of the more than 50,000 Union officers captured from then until it closed on April 2, 1865. All captured Union soldiers brought to Richmond, including the 30,000 enlisted men confined to Belle Isle and 25,000 other enlisted men put in other warehouse prisons, were processed through this building. Since they all passed through, many prisoners claimed they were confined in the notorious building, when actually they were not. Located at Twentieth and Cary Streets, the rear of the 300-foot-long building faced the James River and Kanawha Canal, where supplies and prisoners could be moved by ships. The ground floor contained prison offices, a hospital, and a rat-infested room for those who broke rules. Each of the second and third floors contained three rooms, 103 by 42 feet. The building could comfortably house about 500 prisoners, but the population was sometimes triple that figure.

Libby became the main focus of Elizabeth Van Lew. She began to bring the prisoners books with split spines in which to hide notes, and food on a family platter that had a false bottom in which information could be hidden. She also began a ruse to draw suspicion away from herself. She started wearing clothes common to country folk—buckskin leggings, a one-piece skirt and waist of cotton, topped off with a huge calico sunbonnet. As she walked through the city to and from the prison, she sang nonsensical ditties and mumbled to herself. Soon she was referred to as "Crazy Bet" and considered harmless by many of the guards. But not all the Confederate prison and provost marshal officials were fooled. "I have turned to speak to a friend and found a detective at my elbow,"

Elizabeth noted in her journal. "Strange faces could be seen peeping around the column and pillars of the back portico [of my house]."[27]

The summer of 1862 brought thousands of prisoners as well as thousands of wounded Confederate soldiers to Richmond. Every prison, hospital, and hundreds of homes were filled with the casualties of the Seven Days' Battle. While the great majority of Richmond's society women took care of the wounded Confederate soldiers, making bandages for them and attending their wounds, Elizabeth and her mother did the same for Union soldiers. With the Federals within ten miles of the city, Elizabeth's and her mother's hopes that Richmond would fall were so great that Mrs. Van Lew prepared a room for the Union commanding general, George B. McClellan, to use when he entered the city. But General Lee drove McClellan from Richmond and the war continued.

Meanwhile, Elizabeth looked for further ways to spy on the Confederate government, and soon she developed a plan. One of the family's servants was an intelligent woman named Mary Elizabeth (Van Lew) Bowser. Elizabeth had sent her to Philadelphia to be educated at the Quaker School for Negroes. When she graduated, she married Wilson Bowser. The ceremony took place on April 16, 1861, at St. John's Church, where parishioners were white. The wedding of two blacks at a white church was highly unusual in the South. Miss Van Lew wanted the educated Mrs. Bowser to help her spy, so she persuaded a friend to take Mrs. Bowser to assist at functions at Jefferson Davis's mansion. Elizabeth cautioned Mrs. Bowser to pretend she was illiterate, so as not to arouse suspicion. After several events at the mansion, the friend suggested to Varina Davis that Mrs. Bowser would be a good servant to hire. Mrs. Davis agreed, and the freed slave worked for the Davis family from 1863 until just before the end of the war.

Elizabeth does not reveal in the surviving pages of her journal what information Mrs. Bowser was able to get out of the Davis mansion. But Thomas McNiven, who recruited Richmond loyalists as spies, said Mrs. Bowser was a great help to their efforts.

McNiven worked out of a bakery on North Eighth Street and the Davis family was one of his customers. His memories of that time were recorded by his grandson, Robert W. Waitt: "Her [Miss Van Lew's] colored girl, Mary, was the best as she was working right in Davis' home and [she] had a photographic mind. Everything she saw on the Rebel President's desk she could repeat word for word. . . . She made a point of always coming out to my wagon when I made deliveries at the Davis' home to drop information [off with me]."²⁸

Although Elizabeth had been sending information through the lines for a year and a half, she did not make her first contact with General Benjamin F. Butler, commander of the Army of the James, until late 1863. She sent a message that she was willing to provide him with information. He quickly responded, beginning a series of letters addressed to "My Dear Aunt" and "My Dear Niece," which carried hidden messages. These were revealed when heat and acid were applied to the letters.

Elizabeth was also sending news to other Federal officials. She told them about the difficult times the Confederate army and citizens were having because of the successful blockades of the Southern ports. What could be bought was scarce, and food prices had skyrocketed. "Fast Days" were promoted as a patriotic way of saving on food. "Women are begging for bread with tears in their eyes," she recorded in her journal.²⁹

General George G. Meade, commander of the Army of the Potomac, wrote her on February 4, 1864, using her code name, "Mr. Babcock," to ask if she could get confirmation on which Fredericksburg-area road the enemy wagon trains would be taking to the battlefield.³⁰ Elizabeth destroyed her answer after the war.

While Butler and Meade made their contacts with Miss Van Lew, Colonel Thomas E. Rose and a dozen other Union prisoners at Libby Prison worked on their third tunnel in an attempt to escape. They dug for a few hours each night in a rat-infested room, using a broken chisel and a knife. They covered their work and returned to bed before the cooks were awakened at four o'clock in the morning. Finally the group succeeded in clawing out a 150-foot escape passage. On the night of February 9, 1864, 103 of the prisoners crawled through the tunnel before it had to be closed because of the commotion made by others who wanted to escape.[31] The escaped prisoners headed for safe houses in the city, directions to which had been provided by Miss Van Lew, or toward Williamsburg and the Federal lines. Elizabeth knew that the escape was planned, but the night it took place a family crisis prevented her mansion from being used as a safe house.

Her brother, John, had been a silent partner in Elizabeth's spy efforts, giving her money for the efforts from his hardware business income. But despite having been pronounced unfit because of ill health, he was conscripted in the Confederate army. He was ordered to report to Camp Lee, a few miles west of Richmond. John Van Lew reported as ordered, but deserted within a few weeks. He hid in one of his sister's safe houses, and Elizabeth went there on what turned out to be the night of the Libby Prison escape. Both were fearful, for when they received word the prisoners had escaped, they expected Confederate guards to arrive and search the house. "We were greatly distressed, too, on account of the prisoners; we knew there was to be an exit; had been told to prepare, and had one of our parlors—an off, or rather, end room—had dark blankets nailed up at the windows . . . ; so we were ready for them."[32] But when the escaped prisoners arrived at the Van Lew mansion, the servants feared hiding them without Elizabeth being there. Some, including Colonel Abel Streight, went to other safe houses, where Miss Van Lew met with them the next day.

About the time of the escape, Elizabeth sent Butler what may have been the most important information she gathered during the war. She pleaded for a raid on Richmond to free the thousands of Union prisoners in the warehouses and, most particularly, the enlisted men housed on Belle Isle. At Belle Isle Union soldiers were forced to sleep in the open with little or no covering and were dying at a rate of up to ten per day. More than 400 died during the winter of 1863–64, many of whom froze to death.[33]

Butler felt her information too important for him to act on alone and sent it to Secretary of War Edwin M. Stanton. The war secretary took the information to Lincoln, and a plan was approved to send 3,500 cavalrymen under General Judson Kilpatrick and Colonel Ulric Dahlgren. The raid failed and Dahlgren was killed.

Elizabeth gives a long description of the raid in her journal, but essentially this is what occurred: The Union troops left Spotsylvania Court House, about fifty miles north of Richmond, on February 28. Dahlgren split off with 500 men and headed southwest, planning to cross the James River west of Richmond and to proceed up along the south bank, crossing the bridge to Belle Isle, and freeing the prisoners there. Then he would backtrack to the south bank to recross into the city over Mayo's Bridge to free the prisoners in the warehouses on Cary and Main Streets. Kilpatrick proceeded south to attack the city's northern defenses. When Dahlgren reached the James River, he found it swollen and impassable. He was so angry, he hanged the black scout, Martin Robinson, who had told him he would be able to cross there. Dahlgren then went on a raid, burning farm property, mills, and damaging the James River and Kanawha Canal in Goochland County. Meanwhile, Kilpatrick attacked Hanover Station, north of the city's outer defenses, and alarm bells rang in the city. He was repulsed by the home guard as he neared Richmond, so he turned to the east, looking for another way to enter the city. The home guard also went out the Westhampton Plank Road (now Cary Street Road) to block Dahlgren. Writing after the war, Lieutenant R. Bartley, a signal officer with Dahlgren, told what happened next:

Dahlgren waited till dark, and then came out and formed his men and made the attack, . . . and drove the enemy (who had no artillery) back to the inner line of works, when, reinforcements coming up, it soon got too hot, and he sounded the retreat, leaving forty men on the field, but getting closer to the city than any of our troops ever did up to the day of surrender [of Richmond]. Our column was then turned east and we came round and crossed the railroad at Hungary Station, from there to the Brook pike, and finding from a citizen that Kilpatrick was in retreat down the Peninsula, he determined to cross through King William county and King and Queen county, and try and reach [General Benjamin F.] Butler's lines at Gloucester Point. We crossed the Pamunkey [River] at Hanovertown Ferry.[34]

The Ninth Virginia Cavalry under Lieutenant James Pollard pursued Dahlgren across the Mattaponi River and ambushed him near King and Queen Courthouse. "Dahlgren took the lead, and with his revolver in hand rode close up to the men in the road and demanded their surrender," continued Bartley in his report. "This was answered by a defiant demand on their part for us to surrender. At this Dahlgren attempted to shoot the officer in charge of the Confederates, but the weapon hung fire. Almost instantly a volley was fired into our left flank."[35] Dahlgren was killed and 135 soldiers and forty free blacks were captured. Dahlgren's false right leg and the little finger of his left hand were removed for souvenirs, and his body was dumped in a shallow grave. Reportedly, thirteen-year-old William Littlepage found papers on the body. When the papers were examined in Richmond, they showed that Dahlgren had planned to burn the city and kill President Davis. The news set off an uproar in the government and brought forth condemnation from the newspapers. General Lee wrote that the contents should be published so the world could know of Dahlgren's criminal plans, but he said revenge should not be taken against Dahlgren's men.[36] Jefferson Davis ordered that the body be sent to Richmond. When it arrived in a pine coffin at the Richmond-York Railroad Station, a crowd of civilians pelted the coffin with rocks. Then the body was ordered to be buried secretly outside Oakwood Cemetery, just east of the city. The *Richmond Dispatch* on March 9 proposed that a monument be erected in the city to warn future generations of men like him.

Elizabeth Van Lew made plans with William S. Rowley, another loyalist spy, to steal the body after a freed black, Christopher Taylor, and McNiven watched the secret burial. Elizabeth probably felt responsible for his death. The night of April 5—one month after the burial—the body was removed by the loyalists from the Oakwood Cemetery area and taken to Rowley's farm, north of Richmond.

The body was examined by Elizabeth for wounds, and hair samples were taken from its head. It was then put in another coffin, hidden under three peach trees in a wagon, taken through the Confederate lines, and buried on another Henrico County farm under a peach tree.

Meanwhile, Admiral John A. Dahlgren requested Lincoln telegraph Davis asking for the body of his son. Davis readily agreed and ordered the grave to be opened and the body sent to the family. It was then Confederate officials learned that the body had been stolen. After the war Elizabeth told the Dahlgren family where Ulric's body was buried, and the family retrieved it.

A March 22, 1864, letter from General Butler put Miss Van Lew in what was probably her most precarious situation during the war. He asked her to deliver a request to Phillip Cashmeyer, chief detective under General Winder. The message asked Cashmeyer to meet with General Butler.

In her papers Miss Van Lew described her meeting with a startled Cashmeyer. "As he read [the message] he turned deadly pale. . . . However, he recovered himself and following us out begged me to be prudent and never to come again, saying he would come to see me."[37] Cashmeyer never betrayed Miss Van Lew and continued to see her, which strongly suggests that he too was working for the Union.

In the same letter about the Cashmeyer incident, Miss Van Lew mentioned an unnamed woman who approached her with a basket on her arm and handed her sheets of letters addressed to her, "a communication from the Federal Army asking me to send information at once" on Confederate supplies and where "the sick from hospitals were being sent, etc." Fortunately, she was suspicious of the lady and did not act on the requests. The woman was apparently working for the Confederate provost marshal's office and attempting to set her up. Elizabeth also received a crudely written note threatening to burn her house. It was signed "White Caps,"[38] a group believed to have been a predecessor to the Ku Klux Klan.

Another problem for Elizabeth and her mother was finding money to pay for their spy efforts. An ever increasing inflation was driving up the cost of everything, and they eventually had to sell their cow. It brought $1,500 in Confederate money, only about $75 in U.S. currency.[39]

In May 1864 General Grant began his strategy of striking and sweeping around General Lee's forces from Spotsylvania to Cold Harbor and across the James River to Petersburg. Grant committed thousands of men to hopeless battles at the Wilderness, Spotsylvania, and Cold Harbor. His tactics resulted in an estimated 43,000 dead and injured Union soldiers; at Cold Harbor alone, an estimated 7,000 Union soldiers were killed or wounded in less than ten minutes on June 3.

During these months of terrible fighting, Miss Van Lew continued to send intelligence. "I was able to communicate with General Butler and General Grant," she wrote, "not so well and persistently with General Butler, for there was too much danger in the system and persons. With General Grant, through his Chief of Secret Service, General George H. Sharpe, I was more fortunate."[40] Indeed, once Grant reached City Point, she began to send him not only information, but often a copy of the *Richmond Dispatch* wrapped around a rose from her garden. One of the notes she got through to Butler in November warned that "the enemy are planting torpedoes on all roads leading to the city and fields in front of their line of defenses."[41]

In February 1865 an interesting incident occurred, which Elizabeth duly recorded. A Charles City County farmer, who had been picked up by the provost marshal's office for suspicion of being a loyalist, decided he had had enough of the harassment. Lemuel E. Babcock agreed to help a Federal agent by the name of R. W. Pool (or Pole) get into Richmond, but no sooner had Babcock achieved his mission, when Pool betrayed him to the Confederate authorities. Babcock was arrested and thrown into Castle Thunder. Elizabeth learned of the arrest through an article in one of the Richmond newspapers, but she could not help him. There followed days of suspense until it became clear Pool was not able to incriminate her. Because of Babcock's arrest, Elizabeth's code name was changed from Babcock to Romona, noted McNiven.[42]

On April 2, 1865, President Davis received a telegram while he was at Sunday service at St. Paul's Church. It was from General R. E. Lee, informing him that the defense lines around Petersburg had broken. Richmond was to be evacuated. Word of the news spread rapidly in the Confederate capital.

Government workers piled boxes of papers in the streets and set them afire. Every horse, wagon, and carriage was commandeered to carry important records and the Confederate treasury to the city's Danville Depot. The people were near panic. Jefferson Davis's train left at 8 P.M. The train with the treasury left four hours later. The Confederate rear guard set fire to the tobacco warehouses in Shockoe Bottom to keep their precious commodity from the advancing Yankees. A wind from the southwest, however, swept the burning embers and spread them across the Main Street business district. A fire storm began and hundreds of buildings caught fire. Women ran from their burning houses screaming, and they hurried to the Capitol Square, seeking shelter from the fire. Prisoners escaped from the penitentiary when the guards left. Looters and drunks, racing just ahead of the flames, grabbed everything they could from the stores.

The Union army arrived at sunup the following morning. They took the Capitol and raised the American flag over its sloping roof. Then the Union soldiers formed fire brigades and saved the city from total destruction. A small group of Federal soldiers rode to the Van Lew house in Church Hill to protect it and the family. Elizabeth was not there, but from the house flew a 25-foot American flag she was able to get through the Confederate lines. When soldiers found her that afternoon picking through the ruins of the

War Department building at Ninth and Franklin Streets, she was probably looking for the papers that reportedly had been found on Colonel Dahlgren's body when he was killed. She did not find them in the ashes.

General Butler sent a telegram to Colonel James Allen Hardie, inspector general, recommending he issue a pass to Elizabeth's brother, John, so that he could come home. Elizabeth, Butler said in the telegram, "was my secret correspondent in Richmond. . . . She is now the repository of the secret of the burial place of Col. Dahlgren," he added.[43]

After the war ended, Elizabeth was broke, having spent her inheritance on her spy efforts for the U.S. government. An effort was launched by some of the U.S. Army officials whom she worked with or aided during the war to seek compensation for her from the U.S. Congress.

General George H. Sharpe, chief of the U.S. Bureau of Information (Secret Service), suggested in an 1867 letter to General C. B. Comstock, Grant's aide-de-camp, that Elizabeth be paid $15,000. Sharpe included a letter of support written by General William Raymond Lee, formerly of the Twentieth Massachusetts, who was one of the prisoners Elizabeth aided in Richmond.

Fifteen days after his inauguration as president in 1869, Ulysses S. Grant appointed Elizabeth Van Lew postmaster of Richmond. She received an annual salary of $1,200. The appointment found Northern favor. "We do not suppose that any of the politicians had Miss Van Lew on their 'slates' for Postmistress of Richmond. And yet her appointment by President Grant has given the highest satisfaction to the country," said the *New York Times* on March 21. But in the former Confederate capital, the reaction was the opposite. The *Richmond Dispatch* of March 23 responded to the *Times*'s comments this way: "Please except Richmond—if you consider that a part of the country. We are not at all pleased here. We regard the selection of a Federal spy to manage our post-office as a deliberate insult to our people."

The more that was revealed of what Elizabeth and her mother

did during the war, the more Richmonders had reason to hate her. Her wartime actions, such as paying workers in the arsenal to sabotage munitions, certainly led to the death of Confederate soldiers. Because of her moral belief in the necessity of preserving the Union, she, after all, had betrayed her city.

The people of Richmond showed their disapproval by continuing to treat Elizabeth and her mother as outcasts, as they had during the war. "I live, and have lived for years, as entirely distinct from the citizens as if I were plague-stricken," Elizabeth wrote a friend. "Rarely, very rarely is our door-bell ever rung by any but a pauper, or those desiring my service. . . . September [13], 1875 my mother was taken from me by death. We had not friends enough to be pall-bearers.[44]

Elizabeth ran the Richmond post office for eight years. According to former Confederate general William Carter Wickham, Fourth Virginia Cavalry, she operated the post office efficiently. He wrote in a letter to her dated February 24, 1877: "Your management of the Richmond Post Office has, I believe, been eminently satisfactory to the community here. . . . all my transactions with it, both as a receiver and a transporter have shown me that the office was well handled."[45]

She also received a strong recommendation from outgoing President Grant for reappointment by the incoming Republican administration of Rutherford B. Hayes. "She has filled the post office with capacity and fidelity and is very deserving of continued confidence by a Republican Administration," Grant wrote.[46]

But others, she reported, worked behind the scenes to prevent her reappointment for a third term.[47] They were successful. She was appointed only a clerk and moved to the Washington Post Office by the new administration. Her clerk job lasted just two years. "Her peculiar temperament" made her a "hindrance to the other clerks, and she did come and go at will," wrote the *Washington Evening Star*. Elizabeth had become a "troublesome relict," and should resign, the newspaper added.[48]

She returned to Richmond, out of a job and nearly penniless.

Neighbors treated her like a witch, warning their children not to walk on her side of the street. She spent the next few years writing constantly and angrily to anyone she thought might have influence with the Federal government. She pleaded for a job or compensation for the funds she had spent in her war effort. These letters are written with hummingbirdlike energy: Lines are scribbled across the page, up the sides, and across the top. She seemed to be in constant panic of losing everything, and her anger at being shunned by the Federal government carried over into her dealings with others. John Albee noted in his research that she became a problem at her church, St. John's, constantly coming in late and disrupting the service. She complained, he said, of being "locked out" of the service, and she quit going to church in the early 1880s.[49] She became a constant complainer, offending even her neice, Elizabeth Louise Klapp, who had moved into the Van Lew mansion to help keep house.

Her income having ceased and out of savings, Elizabeth became desperate. As a solution to her financial plight, at one point she apparently considered allowing her journal to be published. In a letter dated July 11, 1887, and addressed to "Gentlemen," she indicated that she had shown part of the journal to a Mr. Brace. "I desire Mr. Brace to know that I objected to writing of myself and parentage because I thought it in coarse taste," she wrote.[50] T. K. Brace was a New York publisher during and after the war.

As a last resort, she wrote of her plight to the family of the late Union soldier Paul Joseph Revere, whom she had befriended in 1862 at the Henrico County Jail. The family and other Northern friends responded with funds to enable her to live out her life in small comfort. Author William Gilmore Beymer identified the contributors as George Higginson, Colonel Henry Lee, J. Ingersoll Bowditch, Frederick L. Ames, F. Gordon Dexter, the Honorable John M. Forbes, William Endicott, and Mrs. George W. Howland, all of Massachusetts. All the men had been Union soldiers, as had Mrs. Howland's husband and son.

Ever the agitator for her causes, she spent her last years arguing

against taxation without representation. With her city tax pay-
ments each year, she sent a note protesting the government's right
to collect taxes from someone who had no right to vote.[51]

On September 25, 1900, she died at home. She was buried
vertically in the family grave at a local cemetery because of the
lack of space. A few family members and friends were present, and
McNiven reported that he knelt at her grave until sundown. Some
years later, relatives of Paul Joseph Revere paid to have a granite
stone sent from Boston and laid at the site.

In her journal she had written the following, which could have
served as her epitaph:

> If I am entitled to the name of "Spy" because I was in the
> secret service, I accept it willingly; but it will hereafter
> have to my mind a high and honorable signification. For
> my loyalty to my country I have two beautiful names—
> here I am called, "Traitor," farther North a "spy"—instead
> of the honored name of "Faithful."[52]

The Van Lew mansion stood unused after Elizabeth's death, except
briefly as the site of the Virginia Club, until it was torn down in
1911 by the city of Richmond. The mansion was replaced with the
Bellevue Elementary School, which is in use today as a model
school.

Elizabeth Van Lew's "Occasional Journal" originally consisted
of over 700 handwritten pages. The last page of the surviving portion is numbered 733. It was buried for a time, however, and many
pages were lost or damaged. In some sections, as many as 50 pages
are missing. In other parts, pages contain large ink spots. What sur-
vives of the journal is about 400 pages. On her deathbed in 1900,
reported John Albee, Elizabeth asked for the journal to be brought
to her. When she saw it, she was disappointed. "Oh, that is not half,"
she exclaimed.[53]

The original journal is housed in the Division of Rare Books
and Manuscripts (Van Lew Papers, Astor Lenox and Tilden Foundations) of the New York Public Library. After reviewing the pages,

I requested a microfilm copy, hoping that pages covered with ink spots could be read with a light behind the film. In many cases the ink-covered words were legible.

In working with the journal, two problems became clear. The surviving pages sometimes do not have numbers, and when there are numbers, there are as many as four. In addition, the events recorded are out of order; to make sense of the journal I rearranged it chronologically.

A first reading of the journal gives the appearance that it was written by two different people. On many pages the words are easily read. But on many other pages the handwriting is like "hen scratch," requiring many readings to decipher the words. After close comparison of the writing, letter by letter, I am convinced it was all written by Elizabeth Van Lew. She was a peculiar woman, quick to react to stress. The hurried writing, or hen scratch, was probably written when she was anxious about being caught recording her part in the spy efforts.

In addition to the journal pages, many letters, notes, road passes, and other mementos have survived the war and are now housed at the New York Public Library and the Virginia Historical Society. These papers include copies of the letters written to her by Generals Butler and Meade during the war. I have included their letters with the journal, inserting them in their appropriate chronological order. The 383 surviving pages of the journal and nearly 100 pages of letters are presented as she wrote them with a few minor inaccuracies, some misspellings, and several unintelligible words. The misspelled words and misused words, such as "tolerant" instead of "intolerant," occur probably because Elizabeth wrote in such haste that her mind was racing faster than she could write. I have used ellipses to indicate where material is missing in the original.

1861

I would if I could give the reader some idea of our daily life during the war, but the keeping of a complete journal was an impossibility and a risk too fearful to run. Written only to be burnt was the fate of almost everything which would now be of value. Keeping one's house in order for government inspection with Salisbury prison[1] in perspective, necessitated this. I always went to bed at night with anything dangerous on paper beside me so as to be able to destroy it in a moment. The following occasional journal, which I take the liberty of inserting in its original form, was long buried for safety, and I therefore ask that its inaccuracies and imperfections may be kindly overlooked and forgiven.

As regards my parentage, I am of Holland Dutch, German and French descent. My father was born at Jamaica, Long Island of Holland Dutch descent on both sides of the same name Van Lew. He was an only son; had one sister who died in marriage. We had an Aunt Letitia Smith Van Lew, whom I have understood was very patriotic during the Revolutionary War and . . . heard interesting stories of her successful labors, etc. for the prisoners, and the fearful scenes of suffering she witnessed in the old church which was used by the British, I believe, as a prison when they occupied New York. . . . My father offended his principal, a Mr. Eisehof, who was very anxious that he should be a professor of Latin and not a merchant which . . . he became when my father came to Virginia. He learnt his business with a Daniel somebody of New York, a prominent man in his day; came when a young man to enter into a partnership with some old citizen by the name of Adams.[2] They failed almost immediately, and left him to begin life with a debt of $100,000 upon his young shoulders. This amount he honorably paid. He was the first person ever to make a hardware business [in Richmond].³

My mother [Eliza Louise Baker Van Lew] was the daughter of German born Hilary Baker, or Hilarious Becker as it was written in his old books. He died in September 1798 of Yellow Fever. He was Mayor of the city of Philadelphia at the time of his death. [He] sent his family out to the farm [he] had next to Stephen Grands on the banks of the Schuylkill River & [he] stayed at his post to minister to the sick & care for the city. There were some family accounts of this sad scene. In this city of his adoption he was taken ill of the fever, taken out to his family & there died by his family. The neighbors w[oul]d bring food etc. & coming for the bussels [in which the food was brought], take them away with tongs. When the end approached, he had his children ab[ou]t. him to give them his blessings. My mother, Eliza Louise, a baby of abt. 3 mon. was put beside him & with her tiny finger stretched, began to play with this great sorrow. So she entered life. Anna Mary, her mother died in 1808. Anna Mary—a funeral notice, I once read, said, in full hope of a glourious [sic] immortality with perfect resignation & without a sign, the remains were removed five years ago, soon after the war [of 1812] because Philadelphia wanted to absorb the grave yard in which they were laid, to Mount Laurel by Mr. George B. Talham, who had married one of the granddaughters. Five of the most tender & touching letters I ever read was [sic] written by my mother when in her forming [sic] this reinterment of her parents. The hand of a little orphan girl had been held. She was old enough, sensitive, intellectual & sympathetic when her mother died to value & love the kinder friend taken from here. She had sisters and brothers whom she loved so, but [they] were married [with] husbands & children. These [facts] came in the poetry [and] stories, which as I said are all for those who like them, of my great grandmother.

My parents were both intellectual & devoted to books. Fifty dollars a yr. was allowed to buy books. Mother had the reading time & when father w[oul]d come home & they had gone to bed, I sometimes, as we slept in the adjoining room, [would] hear [mother's] delicious rehash of all [she had read] for his benefit.

I remember my father coming in at night and waking and taking us up in our long white flannel gowns to sit awhile on his knee; be pressed to his heart, kissed and laid back in our little beds. But the number of years have called and the time passes and passes and can never more come to us. I have seen so much misery often in married life that I am thankful for the memory of one true marriage, blessings we owe more to our parents that we can ever repay. . . . On my maternal side, my mother was of Huguenot [French] descent, and I presume nothing but loyal to a government under which I had seen the blessed light—could have expected of such stubborn stock of Dutch and Huguenot.

From the time I knew right from wrong, it was my sad privilege to differ in many things from the perceived opinions and principles in my locality [Richmond]. This has made my life intensely sad and earnest, and if I may say it tolerant, & uncompromising, but liberal—quick in feeling and ready to resent what seemed to me wrong—quick and passionate, but not bad tempered or vicious. "Daniel and you will see. They shall fall down slain. That is the fulfillment of prophecy." So said with clear eye and bright hope the intelligent colored man, William Roane, that called us owners. And I have heard him draw pictures of his life of freedom never to be realized. William had a bad experience with a Confed[erate]. He was arrested in the st[reet] & when known he belonged to our family the Captors said we'll have you certainly & he worked [remainder of account is missing].

1861

The beginning of the war. There is no denying the fact our people were in a palpable state of war from the time of the John Brown raid. Henry A. Wise was Governor of Virginia,[4] and did everything to keep up excitement, thinking, perhaps, to use his zeal as a stepping stone to popularity and the presidential chain. There were rumors that the whole North was coming. Thousands of men marching in battle array to overwhelm us. The alarm bell would be rung; the tramp of armed men could be heard through the night, and no time was given the people for a sane breath and a perception

of the truth. Such hurry, such haste, such valor, such determination betokened as a ruler either Henry A. Wise or Iron Impotte.
Our people required blood, the blood of all who were of the [John]
Brown party. They thirsted for it; they cried out for it. It was not
enough that one old man should die. No plea of the people intel-
lecting [sic] of misguided youth, would be listened to, and when a
deputation [of loyalists] arrived and waited on the legislature to
solicit mercy for young. . . . Look . . . a lady, one of the most highly
respectable in the city, implored the members to steel their hearts, to
let no appeal, no pity move them! What struck me most painfully
in all this was the universal want of humanity towards the raiders.
I hold that one spark of the love of Christ in our hearts gave us a
feeling of oneness, of sympathy with all his creatures, however
sunken, however sinning. I never thought John Brown right; I have
always thought him one who suffered so deeply with slaves. . . . War,
war in the heart all the while; yet the North would not believe in
our . . . terrible secession.

During the summer of 1860 I was at the White Sulphur
Springs. Mr. [James Johnston] Pettigrew[5] of South Carolina was
there, and Edmund Ruffin,[6] the old man who went South by
request to fire the first gun against Fort Sumter, and whose late
tragic . . . suicide was a fitting commentary of this traitorous act.
I remember his long gray beard and hair, his keen eye, and gentle
form. The political opinions of these two gentlemen differed no
more than their *personnel*. Both men were no more but how different their places in the Nation's memory. The illussolution [sic]
and reconstruction of the Union was the daily talk at the Springs.
There was a military company from Richmond also there and we
had martial music, marching and music even on Sunday. People
were if anything, more morbid than ever on the subject of slavery,
and I heard a member of the Virginia Legislature say that anyone
speaking against it, or doubting its divinity, ought to be hung. Yes,
hung, as certainly and as truly as he would be for murder. Another
gentleman, a state senator, told me that the members of the senate
did not dare to speak as they thought and felt, that they were

afraid, that is, if they did not think pro-slavery or pro-South. He was quite alarmed after making this admission, but I assured him his confidence should not be misplaced or abused. Yet during all this time and subsequently, the sense and heart of the community—the majority of it as all went was for Union. I used to attend the State Convention held in Richmond which afterwards passed the ordinance of secession, and to which they failed to elect the bold and true John Minor Botts. . . .[7] The helm of the State was already in the hands of the traitors. I remember one day seeing old John Tyler, ex President Tyler, with his voice raised for heaven, almost crying, and saying that he had "no influence and was only by courtesy permitted on that floor."[8] The secessionists grew bold and more imprudently daring. All things became worse and worse. Oh, the awe we feel of the coming woe! . . . The doctrine of secessionism seemed to gratify an innate feeling of pride. The women became its strongest advocates, unknowing and unreflecting. "Ah, ladies, when you see your husbands, brothers, and fathers brought home dead, you'll think of this," was said to them on every opportunity by a loyal statesman only to fall as idle words on deaf ears.

I have never yet comprehended the almost universal want of National patriotism among the women. We know very few ladies who were for their Country, very few. In conversation they would become really excited.

I cannot live over again those dark days. I have listened to words of burning eloquence in the Convention; seen the tears in the eyes of many of the members. While at the same time pretty, well dressed ladies of the highest education walk up and down the Capitol square asking, "Do you think the state will go out today for if it does not, I cannot stand it any longer?" Secession flags began now to flaunt from the house tops and from the windows. God help us! Those were sorry days; but the cotton peant [sic] sown in tears was beginning to yield freedom for its harvest.

Drunk with . . . liberty and license our Southern leaders firmly believed in the power of cotton to rule the world. It had clothed and fed them, was it not necessary to clothe and feed all nations!

The first Secession flag, the Palmetto flag,[9] raised by any private individual in the city was flung to the breeze by Brown & Peasley, fishmongers, near the market on 17th Street,[10] with money furnished by negro traders. Just before the Federal army entered Richmond [April 3, 1865], this Brown was much alarmed—told me he expected to be hung for what he had done (and in expectation made over his property to some relative or friend), or that at any note he would be obliged to leave Richmond forever. He expressed contrition and said that latterly he had been doing all he could for the "other side."

Then followed the firing at Fort Sumter. The Convention yet was still, but firm; there was no life in it, so little did this national outrage move it, though the populace were jubilant. The Rebel flag was raised above the Capitol, and there was great ado and some military display, with music, on the square. But John Sescher[11] had not yet signed away his soul, and he came out and ordered the flag to be taken down. The holding of the Convention at Richmond made that city the focus, the soul, the centre of treason. There was also held there what was termed an "Intimidation Convention," which was determined to carry the State out of the Union at all hazards; and to this end had its agents at work throughout the country. The loyal men of the State Convention, intimidated, went over to Secession.

One gentleman, who signed the ordinance of secession, told me he thought that if he had not done so, the streets of Richmond would have run with blood. This same gentleman afterwards told me that, on returning to his constituents, men would come to him weeping and say that they could not vote for secession; that they would take their guns in their hands to the polls and vote for the Union, but he told them they "must vote for secession." I believe if Mr. Botts had been a member of this body he would have been assassinated. This he believed, and told me so. Finally the State was surrendered, and we cried out for the blood of Sumter and Carlisle[12] and the Union members of the convention who fled for their lives. All who had been friendly to them were in danger!

"We shall have war now," said the ladies, joyfully and defiantly, "if Lincoln is not a coward."

Alas for those with loyalty in their hearts, when treason was on every tongue, for those who had been boldly stemming the sweeping current! Many had already formed themselves into volunteer companies. These belonged to the State, and found themselves in the army before they knew it. The whole South became one great military school. We were told that it would only require six per cent of our male population to whip the Yankees, a cowardly set who had only to believe us in earnest to yield [to] all our demands.

Some went so far as to say that one Southern man could whip five hundred Yankees, a race whose extermination, even of women and children, would be a blessing. [Union] General [Winfield] Scott was the object of particular exception.

Brave men were going to Washington to take his sword. Women, ladies, our neighbors, even young girls, took to pistol shooting and firing at a mark.

Now could be seen in the streets [men] with books taking down names of men. Young men were urged to enlist; told that if they did not, they would be drafted and then they would not be . . .

The remainder of this page is missing.

What a memorable day was the 17th of April 1861. How can I describe my feelings when on my way down town, looking towards the Capitol, I saw the flag of treason floating over it. [Governor] John Letcher surrendered the State. I never did remember a feeling of more calm determination and high resolve for endurance over me than at that moment. . . .

In the afternoon of the 19th I was going up town with my brother, [John], when a young girl of fourteen came dancing towards us, exclaiming to some one behind us: "Maria, Oh, Maria. The New York 7th Regiment is all cut to pieces."[13] I stopped her and said, "Little girl, where were you born?" "At the North," she replied, "but I can't help that." Going farther we found the greatest possible consternation and a death-like silence in the streets; people were passing as usual. Men's faces were deadly pale, and little groups could be seen gathering here and there. The first blood had been shed. War in all its reality was upon us, and there were others in earnest as well as ourselves. The news was that Federal troops coming through Baltimore had been attacked and repulsed. We were victorious. There was great profession of joy. "Extras" were issued by the newspapers, and all were to have a torchlight procession that night. The stores were being prepared for an illumination. I saw one man whose eyes flared with the red light of hate. He was reading a paper and thanking God that the negroes, as he said, "had fought on our side." This red light in his eye is willingly burning brilliant, awful to see, to feel, to face.

Just before dark I returned home, bearing on the arm of my friend. I could scarcely see or work for the bitter, blinding tears. My country! Oh, My country! These tears were my feeble offering in atonement for the blood shed in Baltimore.

That night I went to the bottom of the garden to view the torchlight procession. Such a sight! The transparencies with their painted hags; the wicked and blasphemous, . . . the women on foot, the multitude, the mob, the whooping, the tin-pan music, and the fierceness of a surging, swelling revolution. This I witnessed. I thought of France and as the procession passed, I fell upon my knees under the angry heavens, clasped my hands and prayed, "Father, forgive them for they know not what they do!" Mobs went to private houses to hang the true of heart. Loyalty now was called treason, and cursed. If you spoke in your parlor or chamber to your next of kin, you whispered. You looked under the lounges and beds. The threats, the scowls, the frowns of an infuriated community; who can write of them? I have had brave men shake their fingers in my face and say terrible things. We had threats of being driven away, threats of fire, and threats of death. Surely madness was upon the people. Some wished all Union people could be driven into the street and slaughtered. Some proposed the hanging of all persons of Northern birth, no matter how long they had been in the South.

The vote on the ordinance of Secession came in May 1861[14] and was conducted under a system of terror. "Men may vote as they please, but let them dare to vote for the Union, and we will throw them into the river," was said. Now every man feared every man, and distrust was general.

Think of a community rushing gladly, unrestrainedly, eagerly, into a bloody civil war! Imagine how the spirit of evil reigned; the bitter breathing of the fostered hate, the fierce resolve to give to this, proven the sword to find its fury. I know one day I could speak for my country; the next was threatened with death. Surely madness was upon the people! A community with such sins as ours unatoned for, unsheathing the sword of treason; and who think you were chosen to draw the scabbard, the sword which had been fabricating for years with negro traders, with a clergy relying on the protection afforded by their gowns, and with women safe under that of their sex! . . . Public feeling swept all before it, nothing could gainsay it. I saw two young men in tears. They had both joined the army against every principle of their nature. Do you blame them? If you do, then, you don't know that slavery takes away a man's moral or highest courage, and replaces it with that brute valour. . . .

The next two pages of the journal are missing. Chronologically, these thoughts follow:

This heavy heart pulsing and looking upon Slavery as it really is. . . . No pen, no book, no time can do justice to the wrongs it honors. Of this every thinking person born and living in the South, unless precariously situated, must be satisfied. . . Sisters of Charity of Secession feelings had been sent from Baltimore. The R. Catholic Bishop, [John] McGill[15] was for the South as well as the Protestant clergy. Even the Quaker element, with few exceptions, became haters. Mrs. General [James B.] Ricketts[16] can give her experiences of our treatment to herself. She was a true Virginian and devoted to the wounded. Her miseries here. . .

I was a silent and sorrowful spectator of the rise and spread of

the secession mania. I pass over the threats and dangers to which
we were subjected in the unsuccessful attempt made to entrap us! I
once went to Jefferson Davis, himself, to see if we could not obtain
some protection. He was in cabinet session, but I saw his . . . private
secretary, who told me I had better apply to the Mayor.[17]

When the battle of Bethel[18] took place, our papers assured us of a
great victory; that we had lost but one man, a young fellow by the
name of [Henry L.] Wyatt,[19] exceedingly humble in position and
advantages. We made a great hero of him and glory's gory bed was
presented under its most inviting aspects.

From this battle I saw young men returning and heard them
tell how men had tossed the dead Yankees into pits, in a fashion as
"creatures too disgusting to touch." We now began to bring in
prisoners. The tobacco factory in which they were confined was
on Main Street between 25th and 26th streets.[20] And I went to
see them. How my heart beat. There I saw Mr. [David] Todd[21]—
Lieutenant Todd, Mrs. Lincoln's brother. I asked to be made
hospital nurse for the prisoners. He took down my name, looked at
me in surprise, and said I was the first and only lady that had made
any such application. I asked to see the prisoners, but was refused.
I did not know what to do. I called on Mr. [Christopher G.]
Memminger[22] and found him alone in his office in the Treasury
building, the present Custom House.[23] Of him I begged permission to see the prisoners. He looked at me sternly, said he could not
think of such a thing—such a set and such a class, they could
not be worthy or fit for a lady to visit, etc., etc. I told him that
I had once heard him at a convention in peace times speak beautifully on the subject of religion. His face relaxed with a smile. I
said that love was the fulfilling of the law, and if we wished "our
cause" to succeed, we must begin with charity to the thankless, the
unworthy, etc. He therefore gave me a note of introduction to
General [John H.] Winder,[24] to whom I immediately went. I found
him at his shanty office on Bank Street, seated at a table, at which
were two clerks busily engaged in writing, and was most politely

and kindly received. His silvery white hair waved in beautiful locks, and after sitting a moment, I said to him, "Your hair would adorn the temple of James, it looks out of place here." Then I told him I should be glad to visit the prisoners and would like to send them something. He raised no objections, and wrote, "[Miss Van Lew][25] has permission to visit the prisoners and to send them books, luxuries, delicacies and what she may please." How joyful was I to be put in communications with what to me was most sacred—Federal soldiers in prison and in distress!

We had "gone to war in the nick of time" and "the John Brown raid was a God send," said the women. The women all went to work sowing [sic] and knitting, making clothes for soldiers. "Kill as many Yankees as you can for me," was the favor they asked. Mr. Lincoln's head, or a piece of his ear, or some precious relic, was coveted. Charlotte Gorday[26] was our favorite heroine. For once the whole idle South had something to do. Hospitals were put under charge of the women and everything was on a war footing. The arrest of suspected loyalist[s] went on every day.

The troops began to come in from other states; the first division was from South Carolina. It was encamped at the Old Fair Ground, which afterwards became our place for executions; henceforward, let it be holy ground, for there patriots died as gloria.

Oh how heavy was the air with horror! Literally my breathing became labored. My heart seemed cramped! And the poor newly mustered young men! I could not look at them in the streets without the tears coming to my eyes. Hundreds of times during the war, after I learned to know them and their material, did I long to say to them, "be not like dumb driven cattle." We went over to see these troops and found them composed of men belonging to the very humblest chaps and deplorably ignorant. They asked me for "ballard books," meaning hymn books. I dared not speak the truth to them. They told me they had come on to protect Virginia. I asked, "why?" They kindly informed me that Mr. Lincoln had said he was coming down to take all our negroes and set them free, and they were going to protect us women. They also told me this was true—"the newspapers said so." I asked what kind of arms they had. They replied, none; that Virginia was to furnish them.

Receiving personal threats, or being asked and refusing to make shirts for these South Carolina soldiers, Mother and I went again to see them and carried in a large basket a set of "Chambers Miscellanies," a few other books and some flowers. This we considered very innocent "aid and comfort," and it added much to our own comfort. But receiving a letter from one dear to me at the North, inquiring about "Dear Virginia,"

The text skips from page 21 to page 40 on which is written the following:

our ears and startled us with its association of national agony. We were groping in thick darkness. The azure on our flag was gone. The few stars left were set in blood. The shadeless Palmetto, the hissing serpent, types of unrest and treachery, were fitly chosen as our emblems.[27]

The text then skips to page 59.

. . . mistake me, Sir, I mean the lunatic—the insane asylum." "There, there," replied Mr. P., pointing to the different houses in the vicinity. "They are all Insane Asylums; you cannot go wrong."

The leaders now found exciting occupation. Edmund Ruffin, that "white haired patriot and soldier" released from his self imposed exile. . . . a violent secessionist who had been sent to Charleston by the extreme men of the convention to begin the attack upon Sumter was a colonel in the Confederate service commissioned to raise a regiment of infantry.

Henry A. Wise was for action—action, action! Such play making, such speech making in public, in private. Such flag presentations. The drum, the fife, and "Dixie"! For my life, I would not have dared to play "Yankee Doodle," or "Hail Columbia," or the "Star Spangled Banner," our hallowed national airs. The blood-stained Marseillaise resounded through the streets. It had been adopted as the National air. How it fell upon. . .

Some pages are missing here, and on the next existing page of the diary, Elizabeth quotes from an article in the Richmond Enquirer *of July 31, 1861, ten days after the First Battle of Bull Run. More than 600 Union soldiers were taken prisoner and brought to Richmond.*

Two ladies, mother and daughter, living on Church Hill, have lately attracted public notice by their assiduous attentions to the Yankee prisoners confined in this City. Whilst every true woman in this community has been busy making articles of comfort or necessity for our troops, or administering to the wants of the many hundreds of sick, who, far from their homes, which they left to defend our soil, are fit subjects for our sympathy, these two women have been expending their opulent means in aiding and giving comfort to the miscreants who have invaded our sacred soil, bent on raping and murder, the desolation of our homes and sacred places, and the ruin and dishonour of our families.

Out upon all pretexts of humanity! The largest human charity can find ample scope in kindness and attention to our own poor fellows, who have been stricken down while battling for our country and our rights. The Yankee wounded have been put under charge of competent surgeons and provided with good nurses. This is more than they deserve and have any right to expect, and the course of these two females in providing them with delicacies, buying them books, stationery and paper, cannot but be regarded as an evidence of sympathy amounting to an endorstation [*sic*] of the cause and conduct of these Northern Vandals.

1862

An unknown number of pages are missing after the previous entry. The next page concerns the Van Lews taking Captain George C. Gibbs and his family into their home as boarders. He was in charge of Harwood Prison for a brief time at the end of 1861 and the beginning of 1862.

So perilous has my situation become that Mother took Capt. Gibbs & his interesting family to board with us. They were certainly a great protection, but though he had promised us free access to the prisoners, we were not permitted to serve them.

Capt. George Gibbs had succeeded Todd as keeper of the Prisoners. So perilous had our situation become that we took him and his family to live with us..., soon after Mr. Todd was displaced.[1] He [Gibbs] was not a man of much intellect & untidy. "I would give my right arm," I heard him say, "for one word of commendation from Jeff Davis."

The next entry in Miss Van Lew's diary refers to Union officers who were taken from Harwood Prison and held as hostages in the Henrico County Jail for thirteen Confederate privateers captured off New York. Although she does not name them, they were Colonels William Raymond Lee, 20th Massachusetts; Milton Cogswell, 42nd New York; and Alfred M. Wood, 144th New York; Major Paul J. Revere, 20th Massachusetts; and Captains George Rockwood and Henry Bowman, both 15th Massachusetts; and Francis J. Keefer, 1st California. The friend she refers to was Major Revere. Six other Union officers had been transferred to Castle Pickney at Charleston, South Carolina, and they were held in the Charleston Jail as hostages for the privateers.

I visited with a friend in the room occupied by the hostages. Some gentlemen being held as hostages for the rebel privateers. . . . It was a small room with a doubly barred window in a thick wall letting in a sad light to make darkness visible. Aaron Burr[2] had been confined in this prison.

Soon after her visit to the hostages, Miss Van Lew received a notice rescinding her permission to take food to the Union prisoners.

Dr. [Edward G.] Higgenbotham is the Surgeon in charge of the Prison Hospitals and has given orders that nothing to eat shall go into the Hospitals except that furnished by the Commissary of the Post. Acting as his assistant, I cannot violate any order he may give or I would cheerfully oblidge [*sic*] you.

Very Respectfully,
Owen B. Hill
Acting Asst. Surgeon
C. S. Prison Hospital

Jany. 23, 1862
Miss E. L. Van Lew

[I received] a message from Hill of his deep regret; that he had tasted the custard; that it was good and would be beneficial to the sick prisoners, if he could only give it to them, but that he could not do so.

Accompanied by several ladies, the writer [Miss Van Lew] went immediately to the Assistant Secretary of War, Mr. [A. G.] Bledsoe.[3] He said Higgenbotham had no right to refuse; that our prisoners in Washington were most kindly treated and supplied with necessaries and funds by the friends of the South; that it was an assumption of power in Higgenbotham, and he promised to see [Judah P.] Benjamin, Secretary of War, and get permission from him, which I was to send for the next day. To prove the custard innocent of all dirt, I carried it to the war office and left it for the

Honorable gentlemen, hoping it might move them to humanity.
I sent over the next day for an answer and received the following:

Richmond, Jany. 24, 1862
My dear _____
The Secretary of War declined to act on your application
and referred it to Genl. Winder. If I can see Genl. Winder,
I will try to get him to grant your request.
    The custard was very nice, and many thanks to you. I
borrowed some cups from an eating house nearby, and
brought some crackers. So it was eaten in fine style.
                                            Truly Your's,
                                            A. G. Bledsoe

Now I had applied to General Winder, and he did not dare to
interfere in this matter. Already was there a cry against him of
clemency to the prisoners. I was told Higgenbotham hated General Winder, and there was no love lost between them. H. was
placed under arrest by General W., and during his arrest it was easy
to get anything in to the prisoners in the hospitals. I understood
it was for taking precedence in rank that Higgenbotham was
arrested.

*Elizabeth was again given permission by General Winder to take food to
the prisoners. The next sixty-five pages of the journal are missing. It resumes
with her discussion of Libby Prison, which was opened on March 26,
1862, replacing Legion and Harwood Prisons. From that date nearly all
prisoners brought to Richmond were processed through Libby. Most of those
held there were officers, while the majority of the enlisted men were confined
on Belle Isle.*

As regards prisons, the Libby was our best, but I was never permitted to enter it.[4] In the second year of the war I heard Captain Jackson Warner, the commissary, speaking of the prisoners, privates

confined in the tobacco warehouses on Main and Cary streets, say he would rather know that he could not live one week than to live six months on the food these prisoners had; that he could not imagine how they stood it. They used to be served disgustingly. Long before the close of the war, the bread became so intolerable that I cannot conceive how it could have been eaten, unless to kill—corn cobs in small pieces and coarse bran and meal were served out. I brought some of this bread to show hereafter, but mice got to it and after that it bred small bugs which completely riddled it. I should have had it hermetically sealed.

But it was not alone in the matter of food that the prisoners were cruelly treated. They were subjected to brutal violence of the most atrocious description. Private soldiers [Confederate guards] have been known to boast, frequently, that when sent to Richmond from points below with prisoners under their charge, they barbarously butchered these defenseless men; and I know, certainly, of one man belonging to a Virginia regiment, who, having made this assertion, lost neither position nor reputation in consequence. Punishment was never inflicted by the authorities for so flagrant and shocking an abuse of all law. To "lose prisoners" was an expression much in vogue and all understood that it meant cold blooded murder. Yet, we complained of the treatment of Southern prisoners![5]

At Castle Thunder there was an old man, one of the officials, who exhibited the musket, with which he bushwhacked Yankees; yet this mighty and magnanimous Government found but two poor wretches to make examples of. The hanging of [Henry] Wirz[6] was an outrage, making him alone, a helpless foreigner, bear the whole weight of a great government's insults. But there the poor wretch was merely a tool, and had no power of his own. Who vested in him his authority and were responsible for him, and what has been done with them? Dick Turner[7] was the only one who was punished, and he alone suffered confinement. . . .

An undetermined number of pages are missing here. The journal continues with the impending Seven Days' Battle, which lasted from June 25 to July 1.

Friday, June 20, [1862]

How long is this to last? We are in hourly expectation of a battle. It will come when General [George B.] McClellan gets ready. It is said that the two armies have been drawn up in line of battle for two days. (Mother had a charming chamber, with new matting and pretty curtains, all prepared for Genl. McClellan, and for a long while we called [it] Genl. McClellan's room.) We have hatched eight chickens to day, and have a prospect of rearing and eating under our "dear young government," and so we go mincing peace and war. ——— of the Richmond Howitzers and two young men belonging to his company were here on Monday evening. Young ——— from Stafford and young Styles from Connecticut, the son of the Presbyterian minister, Rev. Dr. Styles.[8] Only think of this man's coming off from Conn. with three of his sons, who entered the Confederate service, and leaving his wife and daughters. The little sketch the young man gave me of his own life was exceedingly interesting. He ran away from old Hadley Boarding School when only nine years old; went to sea and did not hear from or return to his parents for two years and a half. Told me his father appeared about the time of a battle. (Styles has a horse and buggy and always turns up at the right moment and gives them valuable information.)

Saturday, June 21, 1862.

The newspapers say that [General P. G. T.] Beauregard and [General Henry W.] Halleck are both expected. Captain [Edward P.] Alexander[9] in charge of battle. [Captain Archibald C.] Godwin[10] told me I had been reported several times. Thursday, the same young man called upon me who was here last winter and made the mysterious appointment—told me he wished to tell me something which would interest me greatly and the government also etc., etc. He came now, insisting, urging us to board him; let him sleep anywhere, in the library, on the floor. We were kind and polite and he took tea with us. We have to be watchful and circumspect—wise as serpents—and harmless as doves, for truly the lions are seeking to devour us.

Thursday, June 26, 1862.
There has been skirmishing for several days. This afternoon I rode
out with Miss Carrington[11] and commodore to Mr. Botts'.[12] The
cannonading was heard more loudly as we progressed. The excitement on the Mechanicsville Turnpike was more thrilling than I
could conceive. Men riding and leading horses at full speed; the
rattling of their gear, their canteens and arms; the rush of the poor
beasts into and out of the pond at which they were watered. The
dust, the cannons on the crop roads and fields, the ambulances,
the long line of infantry awaiting orders. We enquired the news
of the picket who stopped us. He told us that we were whipping
the Federals right, left and in the centre; had taken many prisoners.
The roar of the guns grew louder and louder. We were allowed to
proceed as we were going only a short distance further. We found
Mr. Botts and family listening to the roar of the artillery. The windows rattled. The flash of the bursting shells could be seen. The
roar, too, of musketry could be plainly heard. The rapid succession
of guns was wonderful. The firing seemed to go more around to
the right. About nine o'clock it ceased and with a kind good night
we left our friends; returned by another road; reached home about
ten; found the family much excited, the fight having approached so
near our house that the bursting of the shells could be distinctly
seen from the home window, and the house shook with each
report. No ball could ever be so exciting as our ride this evening.
I realized the bright rush of life, the hurry of death on the battle
field!

*The next two pages in the journal mention an unnamed woman who
caused problems for Elizabeth.*

This woman's bad, ingratitude to me is something. I saw her in a
store, selling a bonnet, a millinery girl, and without a proper home.
I took her home and for months treated her like a lady—a room,
the most desirable in the house, servants to wait on her, & every
attention. Her manner at times was impudent in the extreme, but
judge of my shock and consternation on learning that she had

made an attack on my character, privately, on her leaving the house on Friday.

Elizabeth then mentions the Union spy Timothy Webster. An agent of the Allan Pinkerton Agency, Webster made a number of forays into Virginia to retrieve information. He made his last trip in early 1862, but he became ill while in Richmond. He was arrested by General Winder's detectives, after John Scully and Pryce Lewis, two other agents looking for Webster, were arrested and revealed his identity. Webster was hanged as a spy later that year.

Here Elizabeth also gives her opinions of George W. Alexander, who was in charge of Castle Thunder.

There were two persons of the name of Webster executed—one the Captain [*sic*] Webster to whose death I refer in another place, and the other, Timothy Webster, who was hung as a spy on the testimony of [John] Scully and Pryce [Lewis].[13] When this poor fellow was hung, I went, accompanied by a friend, to Castle Thunder to ask permission for his wife to stay with us. Poor agonized creature. The wife never forget [*sic*] the heartless murder. The introduction of Alexander. No one could look the desperate villain more than this man. Alexander, the keeper of the prison, has written his name high in the annals of cruelty to prisoners. Was a desperate brigand looking villain, and I have heard of him having gold by the bag full. . . . During our visit it was announced that the body of Webster had been brought back and we were politely invited with the poor wife by Alexander to see. I think we could hardly have done this. Alexander would not let her stay with us; said she would be immediately sent off. Took her under his special care, and only when Mr. [William P.] Wood or Colonel Wood[14] of the [Washington, D.C.] Old Capital Prison visited Richmond was she relieved from her sad fate.

The other executed prisoner named Webster was Charles W. Webster, a civilian accused of spying for the Union. Here Miss Van Lew mentions him; George Welch, a Federal soldier; and another spy, Spencer Kellogg.

George Welch[15] was a Federal soldier, who with three of his comrades, was taken prisoner at the time that Capt. Webster [sic] was captured in West Virginia. Webster [was] tried as a spy, but they failed to find him guilty on this charge, and being determined that he should not escape, tried him upon the charge of having violated his parole; upon this he was convicted. After his conviction, he attempted to escape and was recaptured, dreadfully hurt from a fall. So seriously was he injured that he could not afterwards turn over in his bed, yet in this situation he was kept with wrists and ankles shackled, until the surgeon finally ordered them taken off. He was afterwards hung.

George Welch and his companions were brought to Richmond, and all four placed in a very damp, unhealthy cell in Castle Thunder. It was evidently the intention of the authorities that they should never get out alive. They were treated with extreme severity, not allowed to leave the cell. Pining and wasting under starvation and abject misery, three of the four died one after another. Welch alone survived a confinement of thirty-one months in these wretched dens, for dens they were. It is believed that these men were applied for by the United States government, and the answer was given that they were not here. There were no charges against them, no evidence of any thing wrong; they never had a trial, nor was there any earthly reason why they should not have been treated as prisoners of war. Welch escaped through the clerk of the prison putting his name by bribery by mistake upon the list of those to be exchanged, and he was sent off before the mistake was discovered. During his lengthy confinement he had been kept in irons. . . .

Very different was the fate of Spencer Kellogg,[16] whom we executed as a spy. He had rendered service which caused the fall of New Orleans, and entered the fort as an engineer; had been enabled to communicate valuable information. Before leaving the prison, he drew from his finger a ring and sent it with a message to his young wife, to whom he had been married but three or four weeks when he undertook the dangerous mission, which terminated in his death. He was an educated gentleman, sustained by firm Christian faith, and went to the gallows glorying in his fate and in being worthy to die for his country.

On the way to the peace of execution, followed by the crowd to see him die, he looked towards them, and then asked one who accompanied him, "did you ever pass through a tunnel under a mountain? My passage, my death, is dark, but beyond all is light and bright." This language is not exactly remembered, but it was beautiful. He spoke of the flowers and of glory in an already translated state.

The last comments in the 1862 portion of Elizabeth's diary are unclear. In the first comment she says that the "press" so inflamed "the people" that no one—presumably none of the loyalists— "was allowed to visit the [Union] prisoners." A review of the local newspapers for July does not show any inflammatory articles. Nor does John Beauchamp Jones, the Confederate War Department clerk who kept a detailed diary of goings-on in Richmond during the war, mention any situation as described by Elizabeth. In the second comment Elizabeth made reference to a letter written to a "New England man of our city" in which the writer asked that the "New England man" do something for a Southern soldier. She says the letter was published "in the paper," but no letter was found in the review of the local newspapers. There also are no records existing concerning the ten U.S. soldiers she mentions being moved to Castle Godwin prison. Her comments were these:

About the last week in July, the press so inflamed the people & people became so violent that no one was permitted to visit the prisoners or do any thing for their relief. And the articles in the papers speak of their [the Union prisoners] being ministered to by our people & the kind hand of women—Were altogether sheer fabrications, *fancy sketches* drawn from the imagination. In peril and powerless were all—And a New England man of our city, written to by a friend to do something for a prisoner who the Northern friend w[oul]d. [the next words are unclear]—was replied to at length in a long letter, which was published in the paper—it was inhuman and disgraceful. I said that his conscience & principles w[oul]d not permit him etc. That they [Southern prisoners] were receiving better treatment than they minister etc. And I heard of another gentleman of high position who expressed himself insulted at a similar letter.

In Aug. ten U.S. soldiers, who had been captured, were taken from the Libby—& put in C. G. [Castle Godwin] in a room ab[ou]t 10 × 12 feet in size containing one door & a window. A physician[,] temporarily health officer at the prison[,] gave me the following description in fact.

The remaining pages of 1862 are missing.

1863

Few entries survive from 1863. Most likely the other pages were lost or destroyed; nearly half of the journal is missing. The first existing entry concerns the Van Lews' horse and the state of the Confederate army, which needed horses and men to replace its losses.

Upon two occasions we were obliged to put in a substitute for our horse. This little business of substitution cost us much, and after the last time the Government refused to give us protection papers for him. There was no safety "for man or beast" in our "dear young Government."

During raids or panics, I have known them to take the horses on the street from a bread cart, from country carts coming to market, though they publicly advertised that this would not be done. Frequently not a horse was to be seen on the streets, except those in Government employ.

Horses found strange hiding places. We hid ours for several days sniffing the smokehouse air, but they traced him, so we spirited him into the dwelling house, spread straw upon the study floor, and he accepted at once his position and behaved as though he thoroughly understood matters, never stamping loud enough to be heard, no neighing. This was his hiding place several times, sometimes for a week together. A good loyal horse, and the Yankee advent found him in his Sanctum [when they arrived April 3, 1865].

The second remaining 1863 journal entry is a rambling discourse on the treatment of slaves.

There were two distinct codes governing master and slave—one called the white code and the other the black. The negro, the one always to go by the board, and the indians say, "Indian first, dog next, nigger last."

A gentleman once said to Bishop Polk,[1] when he [the gentleman] was working 200 negroes, "I do not believe that any man get [sic] to heaven who has the immediate control of 200 slaves," and asked his opinion. The bishop answered that he was "not prepared at that time to give an answer but would think about it."

A minister from the pulpit thus addressed his congregation. "I have asked if it is not a sin for us to cheat the feelings of hatred unto the enemy? I answer now," drawing himself up to full stature, "tremble in your answer & go to the battle field & there defend your friends, etc." This was from a popular clergyman. . . .

The poor creatures [blacks]—punishment for any little thing, misdemeanor or stubbornness. They would be placed in a coffin with holes over their face to breathe through, and keep them in here from 24 to forty hours. Then there were the blocks, upon almost every place of which I could attempt no description, the beatened slaves is too horrid to believe, unless one had seen it. What I write I can prove. Negroes whipped almost to death in Louisiana. If the law becomes cognizant of it, [it] takes the negro from the master as punishment to the master, & sell[s] him to another who has full whipping powers. There is not one negro in 1,000 who has knowledge that in a certain no. of slave holders with hate. . . . Death & whipping w[or]k was all the negro got, and in Louisiana a politician sent in a bill to abolish sending negroes to the penitentiary on the ground that a negro was better off in the penitentiary than at home under his master. Have we mentioned handsaw whipping? Handsaw, which grazed the skin, was one other method of punishment. A Buck skin is raw hide, lash until the man whipping would have to draw only through his finger as if milking to rid it of the blood. Negro whips. The blood would be in puddles where they whipped. These Negro whips were made of the North cowhides & all & sent south. . . .

*Near the end of 1863, Elizabeth sent a messenger to General Benjamin F.
Butler, commander of the Army of the James. Her message precipitated his
December 19 inquiry to see if she would work for him as a spy or "corre-
spondent." He wrote the letter from his headquarters at Fortress Monroe.*

Dec. 19, 1863 Commander Boutelle,[2] U.S. Coast Survey
Office, Washington, D. C.
My Dear Boutelle: You will find enclosed a letter from a
friend of yours in Richmond. I am informed by the bearer
that Miss Van Lieu [*sic*] is a true Union woman as true as
steel. She sent me a bouquet, so says the letter carrier.

Now, I much want a correspondent in Richmond, one
who will write me of course without name or description
of the writer, and she need only incur the risk of dropping
an ordinary letter by flag of truce in the Post Office in
Richmond, directing to a name at the North. Her messenger thinks Miss Van Lieu will be glad to do it.

I can place my first and only letter in her hands for her
directions, but I also place the man's life in her hands who
delivers the letter. Is it safe so to do? Will Miss Van Lieu be
willing to either correspond herself or find me such a correspondent? I could pay large rewards, but, from what I
hear of her I should prefer not to do it, as I think she would
be actuated to do what she does by patriotic motives only.

I wish therefore you would write me, confidentially—
and as so much is depending, in the strictest secrecy, what
you think of the matter. Of course you will readily see that
I can furnish means by which a very commonplace letter
on family affairs will read very differently when I see it.

Truly yours, Benj. F. Butler[3]

1864

Elizabeth agreed to Butler's request to spy for him. The general sent his first letter to her January 18, 1864.

My Dear Aunt: I suppose you have been wondering why your nephew has not written before, but we have been uncertain whether we should be able to send a letter. The Yankees steal all the letters that have any money in them through Flag of Truce, so that we thought we would wait until we got a safe chance.

I am glad to write that Mary is a great deal better. Her cough has improved, and the doctor has some hope. Your niece Jennie sends love, and says she wishes you could come north, but I suppose that is impossible. Mother tells me to say that she has given up all hopes of meeting you, until we all meet in heaven.

Yours Affectionately, James Ap. Jones

After heat was applied to the letter, this message appeared:

My Dear Miss: The doctor who came through and spoke to me said that you would be willing to aid the Union cause by furnishing me with information if I would devise a means. You can write through Flag of Truce, directed to James Ap. Jones, Norfolk, the letter being written as this is, and with the means furnished by the messenger[1] who brings this. I cannot refrain from saying to you, although personally unknown, how much I am rejoiced to hear of the strong feeling for the Union which exists in your

own breast and among some of the ladies of Richmond. I
have the honor to be,

>   Very respectfully, Your obedient servant.

*Elizabeth's next existing journal entry is dated January 24, 1864. It
mentions the shortage of food in Richmond.*

Alas for the suffering of the very poor! Women are begging for
bread with tears in their eyes, and a different class from ordinary
beggars. What an experience is that of an intelligent person, born
and brought up in the Southern States, and continuing their residence there through this terrible rebellion. The peace, plenty, and
freedom of the whites under the old government stands in strange
contrast with the scarcity and apprehension of the Southern Confederacy Government. On Thursday I went through the city for
meal and could not get a particle any where. I went to the City
Mills. They told me they had no corn and could procure none.
They were only grinding for toll, as persons would bring them
corn; that "the people" would come crying to them for meal and
they did not know what to do; that they had none to give them
and people must starve. The miller told me they were grinding at
the little mill on the Dock.[2] I went immediately there and found it
so, but they would let no one family have more than a peck at any
price. There were crowds of persons coming and going, each for or
with their peck, and for this peck they paid five dollars, which was
cheap. I tried to get rice, but we could not. We bought one hundreds pounds for fifty dollars a few days since. Friday we bought a
bushel of meal for $225 per barrel. There is a starvation panic upon
the people. I do not think it is yet as desperate as many imagine,
but in all this there is great consolation. I am willing to live on
crust, to give up everything, provided everything is taxed and
taken from every body else. No boy over fourteen is permitted to
leave the "Confederacy." I meet everywhere the unplaned, rough
coffins of the wretched prisoners.

This portrait of Elizabeth Van Lew was first published in the 1912 book *On Hazardous Service,* by William Gilmore Beymer. The original source of the wartime photograph is not known.

Elizabeth Van Lew, "Crazy Bet," as she looked during the Civil War. She was forty-three years old when the war began. *Painting courtesy of the Library of Congress*

Elizabeth Van Lew was shunned by Richmond society until her death in 1900 because of the help she gave the Union during the war. This photograph was taken when she was seventy-six years old. *Photo from the* Boston Morning Journal, *October 2, 1900*

Elizabeth Van Lew, *right,* had dinner with·her brother, nieces, and nephew in the garden. Others in the photograph are her brother, John Newton Van Lew; his daughters, Annie Randolph Van Lew *(seated to her father's left),* Eliza Louise Van Lew *(seated on Elizabeth Van Lew's right);* and his son, John Van Lew. The empty chair, *center,* was placed at the table in memory of John Newton and Elizabeth Van Lew's mother, who died a year before this photograph was taken in 1876. The black servant is not identified. *Photo courtesy of the New York Public Library and Archives*

Elizabeth Van Lew is shown in this photograph in her later years sitting in the garden of the Van Lew mansion. *Photo courtesy of the Library of Congress*

A page from Elizabeth Van Lew's diary shows a handwriting that was much like "hen scratch." She wrote up and around the pages, as well as across. Ink spots marred a number of pages of the diary. *Photo by the author. Diary page courtesy of the New York Public Library and Archives*

Thomas McNiven, *standing,* ran the Yankee spy network in Richmond for the Union Secret Service. McNiven came to Richmond from New York and used a Richmond bakery as a front for his spy operations. He recruited spies from the Richmond City Council, the Confederate government, and local citizens. Although Elizabeth preferred to work mostly with her own recruited spies, she and McNiven also worked together. Shown with McNiven is his brother, John, who was a Union soldier. *Photo courtesy of Robert W. Waitt*

William Rowley, a Henrico County, Virginia, farmer, was one of Elizabeth's spies. He was instrumental in hiding Union Colonel Ulric Dahlgren's body in 1864, after Elizabeth's loyalist friends stole the body from an unmarked grave. *Photo from the book* On Hazardous Service

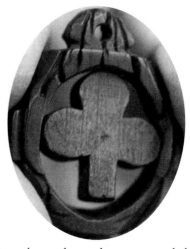

Carved peach seeds were used by McNiven's and Elizabeth's spies to identify each other. When the hinged clover in the center of the seed was turned up, it was unsafe to talk. Women wore them on their dresses and men on their watch chains. *Photo by the author. Peach seed courtesy of Robert W. Waitt*

Union Colonel Ulric Dahlgren, *standing,* led a raid on Richmond in 1864 to free Union prisoners. The raid was a failure and Dahlgren was killed. His body was stolen from a Richmond grave and buried under three peach trees on a Henrico County, Virginia, farm. The body was returned to the Dahlgren family after the war. *Photo courtesy of the Library of Congress*

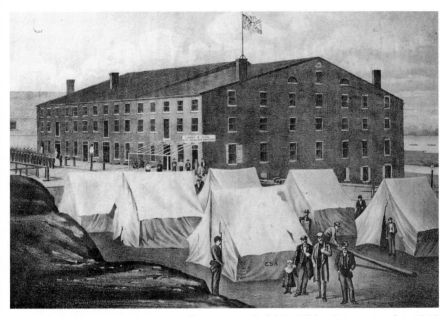

Thousands of captured Union officers were held in Libby Prison. In this 1863 drawing, prison officials pose in front of the prison. They were identified as William D. Turner, the son of prison policeman Richard Turner; Sergeant Erasmus Ross, prison clerk; Richard Turner; and Thomas P. Turner, commandant of Confederate prisons. After Ross's death in the fire at Richmond's Spotswood Hotel in 1870, it was revealed that he worked for Elizabeth Van Lew. He had played his part as a vile, cruel Confederate soldier so well that when Union soldiers took Richmond on April 3, 1865, Ross sought protection at the Van Lew mansion. He feared the Union soldiers would hang him. Unknown to most of the Union prisoners, Ross had helped free some of them. *Drawing courtesy of the Library of Congress*

This painting by a prisoner, Major Otto Botticker, shows his fellow captives housed in Libby Prison in 1862. Some slept, some played chess, but all wanted to go home. *Painting courtesy of the Anna S. K. Brown Collection, Brown University*

In 1864 Union prisoners succeeded in digging a tunnel from Libby Prison. The author's research of Union Prisoners' Unit Records and National Archives records confirmed that 103 prisoners escaped through the tunnel on February 9, 1864. *Drawing courtesy of the Anne S. K. Brown Collection, Brown University*

Colonel Thomas E. Rose, 77th Pennsylvania, led the Libby Prison escape. He was later recaptured near Williamsburg. *Drawing courtesy of the Library of Congress*

After exiting the escape tunnel, Union officers headed east from Richmond toward Williamsburg as they attempted to reach the Union lines. *Drawing courtesy of the Library of Congress*

Richmond burned on April 3, 1865, after a fire set by retreating Confederate soldiers raged out of control. When Union soldiers arrived that day, they put out the fires and saved the city from ruin. *Currier & Ives painting courtesy of the Library of Congress*

The American flag flies over the Virginia capitol building on April 3, 1865. In the foreground are burned-out buildings along the city's waterfront. *Photo courtesy of the Library of Congress*

Elizabeth Van Lew was buried in the Van Lew family plot in Shockoe Hill Cemetery. The stone placed over her grave was paid for by relatives of Union soldiers she had helped during the war. *Photo by the author*

Many loyalists in Richmond attended St. John's Church, which was conveniently close to Elizabeth's house. She and her associates also met at the church, wearing peach seed pins, to exchange information. This 1865 photo shows neighborhood children by a Union ambulance wagon near the church. *Photo by Mathew Brady, courtesy Library of Congress*

A man told me to day that he knew for a certainty and of his own knowledge, that the commissaries had the beef sent to the prisoners from the United States and withheld it from them, giving them our beef, and that the Confederate coffee was substituted for real coffee. The officers, surgeons, stewards, etc. using the latter. That the prisoners received the rice sent to them. The sick prisoners are suffering for covering, and dying, it is said, of dysentery, but in reality of starvation. I cannot go to church. I went last of all to the Friends' Meeting, and heard the preacher, ————, pray, "God, bless the Confederate Congress." This I could not do.

Many prisoners on Belle Isle were dying, some from malnutrition and others freezing to death from lack of warm clothing. Union army regiment records show that more than 400 Federal prisoners died at the island prison or from illnesses contracted there during the winter of 1863–64. Elizabeth sent the following letter to General Butler:

January 30, 1864
Dear Sir: It is intended to remove to Georgia very soon all the Federal prisoners; butchers and bakers to go at once. They are already notified and selected. Quaker,[3] a Union man whom I know, knows this to be true. Are building batteries on the Danville road.

This from Quaker: Because of new and rash council! Beware! This I send you by direction of all your friends. No attempt should be made with less than 30,000 cavalry, from 10,000 to 15,000 infantry to support them, amounting in all to 40,000 or 45,000 troops. Do not underrate their [the Confederate's] strength and desperation. Forces could probably be called into action in from five to ten days; 25,000, mostly artillery. [General Robert H.] Hoke's and [General James L.] Kemper's brigades gone to North Carolina; [General George F.] Pickett's in or about Petersburg. Three regiments of cavalry disbanded by General

Lee for want of horses. [General John Hunt] Morgan is
applying for 1,000 choice men for a raid.

*Elizabeth followed the above entry with the conversation between her mes-
senger and General Butler on February 4. She may have been provided a
copy of the conversation by Butler, for he also recorded it in his papers.*

General: "Well, my boy, where did you get that letter from?" "Miss
Van Lew gave it to me. I stayed for a week with Miss Van Lew
before I came away. Miss Lizzie said she wanted to send you a letter, and I said I would bring it. Miss Lizzie said you would take
care of me. I left there last Saturday night. Miss Lizzie told me
what to tell you."

General: "Well, what did she tell you to say? You need have no
fear here."

"She told me to tell you the situation of the army. Mr. Palmer[4]
got all the information he could for you. Lee has got about 25,000
men; there are about 15,000 men at Petersburg. The City Battalion
and two companies are at Richmond, and about 1,800 or 2,000 at
Chaffin's and Drewry's Bluffs.[5] Mr. Palmer said there were two
brigades gone to North Carolina about a week before I left. He
found out, though, just before I came away, that one of them had
stopped at Petersburg. The two brigades that went were Hoke's
and Kemper's. He thought that what available force could be got
into Richmond in four or five days was from 25,000 to 30,000
men. He said to say to you that Richmond could be taken easier
now than at any other time since the war began. He thought that
it would take about 10,000 cavalry and 30,000 infantry."

General: "Miss Van Lew says something in her letter about
Quaker."

"There is a man there goes by the name of Quaker. That is not
his name, but he says he does not wish any one to know his name;
he does not wish to be known by any other name. They are sending
off the Federal prisoners to Georgia. Mr. Palmer said he had understood that Lee was there in Richmond in secret session there, but he

said that was not reliable. Lee has about 25,000 available men. Miss Van Lew said not to undervalue Lee's force. Quaker said his plan to take Richmond would be to make a feint on Petersburg; let Meade engage Lee on the Rappahannock; send 200 or 300 men and land them at the White House[6] on the other side of Richmond, so as to attract attention; then have 10,000 cavalry to go up in the evening, and then rush into Richmond the next morning."

General: "How did you get through?"

"Mr. Holmes[7] got a man to bring me to guide me. He paid him $1,000 in Confederate money, and he brought me to the Chickahominy and left me there. He fooled me. I came across the river. I got a boat. I don't think there are any men on the Chicka-hominy, or only a few cavalry. There are none nearer than Lee's army. At Chaffin's farm[8] there is about a regiment. He told me to tell you that Drewry's Bluff is the strongest point; he said you must come around Richmond on the other side. Morgan is applying for 1,000 men. The papers say he is going to make a raid into Ken-tucky. I don't believe that, though, for if he was, the papers would not say so. Miss Van Lew said that all the women ought to be kept from passing from Baltimore to Richmond. She said they did a great deal of harm. She also said that there was a Mrs. Graves[9] who carried a mail through to Portsmouth. She hoped you would catch her. The last time she brought a mail into Portsmouth she came in a wagon selling corn."

General Butler sent Elizabeth's January 30 letter and a record of his con-versation with her messenger to Secretary of War Edwin M. Stanton. He added his own letter February 5:

Hon. E. M. Stanton, Secretary of War

I send enclosed for your perusal the information I have acquired of the enemies' forces and dispositions about Richmond. The letter commencing, "dear sir," on the first page is a cypher letter to me from a lady in Richmond with whom I am in correspondence. The bearer of the letter brought me a private token showing that he was to be trusted.

There are not now in Lee's army or about Richmond thirty thousand men. I can get no co-operation from [General John] Sedgwick.

Forty thousand men on the South side of the James would be sufficient for the object of taking and permanently holding of Richmond. The roads have been good up to to-day. You will see that the prisoners are to be sent away to Georgia. Now is the time to strike. On Sunday I shall make a dash with six thousand men,[10] all I have that can possibly be spared. If we win, I will pay the cost; if we fail, it will be at least an attempt to do our duty and rescue our friends. . . .

The next entry is a February 4, 1864, note from Union General George G. Meade, commander of the Army of the Potomac. It is the only item in the surviving journal that gives Elizabeth's code name Babcock. That she did not destroy the note is a mystery, for if it had been discovered, it would have resulted in her arrest and perhaps death.

Head-Quarters, Army of the Potomac,
2 P.M. Feb. 4, 1864
Mr. Babcock—
Have you any confirmation being over what roads the enemy move their supply wagons from Battlefield?

Geo. G. Meade
Maj. Genl.

Elizabeth's response was apparently in the papers she retrieved from the War Department on December 12, 1866, and destroyed.

On the night of February 9, 1864, 103 Union prisoners escaped through a fifty-foot-long tunnel dug from Libby Prison.[11] Elizabeth had gone to visit her brother the night of the escape. He was in hiding after deserting from the Confederate army.

My brother was about to go through the lines when the prisoners escaped through the tunnel. This redoubled the vigilance of the guards & made escape impossible [for her brother] the night of that memorable exit. I had disguised myself in coarse clothes—with a sunbonnet on my head & a basket on my arm. I had no appearance of myself, but I was overcome with the thought that maybe it wasn't a disguise to others—I was & appeared to myself my own proper person & that it [the disguise] would require presence of mind & casual appearance. I persuaded another to prevent betrayal of self—thus a singular thing & feeling & worthy of notice.

I went to the kind family where my brother was located. They were poor & I passed the night with them. My brother slept in the room above with the husband, & I with the wife in the lower room. I shall never forget the nice clean sheet, the courteous attention & my first lying with them. The wife took her pipe, lighted it, & puff, puff, puffed until ready to retire. I could not sleep, the novelty of my situation & the pipeing [sic], and my anxiety added to a strange nervousness or presentment [sic] filling my mind. In the morning our driver came out with a basket full of supplies. As soon as he called, he said that there was great trouble & excitement; that brother was in great danger; that many prisoners had escaped during the night; and that some had come to his door—the door to the servants' room on 24th St—and asked for Col. [Abel] Streight [one of the escaped prisoners], & begged to come in, but that he was afraid they were not prisoners, only our own people in disguise to betray us & would not let them in. That some had stood off, by the corner of the [St. John's] church and wall, & watched & he was afraid that he was late in getting to us because he had to go so much out of his way & so far around to come safely. Brother then had to give up all hope of escape because we knew vigilance would be redoubled & we were in great trouble for the loyal family that he was with because it was to be expected their home would be searched & it would have gone very hard with them had a deserter been found secreted there. We were greatly distressed too on account of the prisoners. We knew there was to be an exit, had been told to prepare, & had one of our parlors or rather end rooms—had dark blankets nailed up at the windows & gas had been kept burning in it—very low day and night—for about 3 weeks. We were so ready for them, beds prepared in there. I returned home, after going as quickly as I could, in despair.

As desperate situations sometimes require despicable remedies, I determined to go to Genl. Winder. As I went up town I saw the men mounted on horseback, three abreast, scanning the town & going on to the vicinity for the poor and fleeing prisoners. Genl. Winder received me kindly. I told him I was in trouble & had come to him; & then that my brother had been enscripted & was deserted, & was secreted. "He should not have," said the old gentleman, "but bring him to me tomorrow morning. I will do what I can for him."

I went with my brother to him. Genl. Winder, after talking with him & examining him, being satisfied that from an injury he was suffering from, he was not fit for service, told him that he would see early the examining physician & attend himself, & do all he could for his exemption, telling him when to come again. When my brother next went, Genl. Winder said, "I am sorry, but I could have no effect with the Ex. Dr.," & repeated what they said. "Now Mr. Van Lew that is the best I can do for you." He then wrote to Col. [Henry E.] Peyton at Camp Lee, that he would oblige him [Winder] by giving Mr. Van Lew 3 days furlough, & permit him to choose a regiment. Then, "Mr. Van Lew I wish you to choose your company—choose the 18th VA Regt.; that is mine & I can protect you."

I went with my brother to the conscript camp. Col. Peyton was much displeased & did some cursing to my brother; refused to give 3 days, but two, & permission to choose his Regt. I think this choice was not to be made until the furlough expired. [Here, Miss Van Lew wrote a note to herself to "put in what I have written or rather refer to it." Her note is unclear.] On our return we went together to the law office of a friend ———— Roberts.[12] He was told what had occurred & of the discourtesy of the Confed. officer Peyton, & began talking that it was not to be expected that when men were risking their carcasses that such as we should be tolerated, etc. . . . The prisoners were being recaptured, our own family torn with anguish, & before I knew it, I said, "It is a damned rotten concern, & I pledged myself to do all I can against it." There needed no guarding angel to blot this out, & I tried faithfully to keep my word. This little drama removed, [I] let out my pent up feelings—judge me only those who have been judged. Genl. Winder was as good as his word. My brother secured a Confederate uniform & reported to duty & that was the great panic day. The man on guard duty before the door was old, & the Capt. told brother he had better take the musket from him & take his place for a time, which he did. I went once to try to bribe Genl. Winder, to get my brother off—offered good Confederate dollars—but the old gentleman was offended & told me never to make any such proposition again.

Mrs. Winder told mother that the Genl. said it was a clear case of usual animosity to the [Van Lew] family. My brother had the friendly feeling of the company, but I think it cost him one hundred dollars in come back and whiskey which much affects the feelings. I have no reason to believe Genl. Winder was corrupt. The [Winder] family had very plainly recognized & tried very plainly upon the occasion they dined with us. I attempted to talk Southern Confederacy. Upon leaving the room, brother came after me & said, "for God's sake sister do not try to talk it—it is the most bitter kind of irony." Mrs. Winder told mother that she was greatly distressed at the breaking out of the war & said other strong things which always made mother believe that she, Mrs. Winder, had a strong feeling for the U.S. gov. She was a mature woman. Miss [Caroline Ann "Connie"] Eagles, her daughter, was intensely disloyal, but Mrs. Winder told mother that Genl. Winder was distressed at the feeding of the prisoners at Andersonville, but not able to do better for them. [Phillip] Cashmeyer from Baltimore was Genl. Winder's

head detective. He told me of his own want of means some months
after the closing of the war & was in Washington, & one of the Gov.
special agts. named me.

*Union Colonel Abel Streight, Fifty-first Indiana, said during an interview
after the escape that Miss Van Lew hid him in her house.*[13] *Streight was
mistaken; he was hidden in the house of one of Elizabeth's friends.*

I shall ever remember the 15th of February, 1864 because of a great
alarm I had for others! Colonel Streight and three of the prisoners
were secreted near Howard's Grove.[14] After passing through the
tunnel, they were led by a Mrs. Greer[15] to a humble house on the
outskirts of the city. There Mrs. Rice[16] received them. She waited
upon them herself, though in poor health—walking to and from
town. Peril and fatigue she courted now so they might escape their
prisons. By request of some of their members she came to see them.
(This place is thickly settled and in this plain neighborhood any display of equipages would create an excitement.) I followed Mrs.
Rice into the house, the front door of which opened into the parlor or sitting room, and I found myself in the presence of the four
fugitives. I was overcome with terror for them that I quite lost my
voice for some time. Two of these gentlemen were quite sick and
looked very feeble. Colonel Streight seemed in good condition.
I mentioned that there was particular enmity towards him, because
he had commanded, it was said, a negro regiment. He replied, "I did
not, but would have had no objection." He asked me my opinion of
the cause of this war. I tried to say, Democracy, though in my heart
I thought it was slavery. I had a very pleasant visit. How my
heart ached all the while for their peril!

I was particularly delighted with the man who made the tunnel—Col. McDonald, I think, was his name.[17] Broad shouldered
and kind hearted, an honest, true genial looking man; it was a
pleasure to take the hand which had worked so faithfully, so hard,
to deliver himself and fellow prisoners. He put in my hand the
chisel with which alone he made the passage. I wanted him to

leave it with me to take care of for him, but he preferred carrying it with him. Our people were showing a tin sugar scoop, and say that the work was done with that alone. By this ingenious tunnel, 109 prisoners escaped, 65 of whom were recaptured.[18] Their escape was not known until 8 o'clock. (I have heard since that Col. McD was killed in battle. I hope this is not true.)[19] We had a little laughing and talking and then I said good bye, with the most fervent, "God help you," in my heart towards all of them. Mrs. Rice came home with me. We were afraid of the hack driver, and he took advantage of it to ask a round sum in Confederate dollars. It was not safe for me to go again to see these gentlemen, but I heard from them through Mrs. Rice. I felt troubled about my reply to Colonel Streight, and I wrote him a note which I entrusted to one to hand him, but after he left, it was returned to me. Here it is:

You asked me my opinion of the cause of this war, and I do not feel satisfied with my reply, for it was not the truth, as it appears to my mind, but the opinion of one whose intellect I much respect—Mr. Botts. He has endeavored to convince me that Democracy was the whole and sole cause, but I always told him I thought it was slavery. In this belief my head and heart agree. Slave power crushes freedom of labor. Slave power is arrogant—is jealous and intrusive—is cruel—is despotic—not only over the slave, but over the community, the State. Slave power was losing this strength before the increasing influence of honest and enlightened free labor. I think this is one of the most deeply interesting of questions, but cannot enter into it now. It is a vast field in which I have gathered many facts. I have thought and felt deeply on this subject. I would be glad to speak with you, but the time is not now. I beg that you will [not] send me the pamphlet or book you spoke of having written, unless you want to have my head taken off by the powers that be, but be so kind as to remember me, and if after this war it pleases you to send it, I should be much gratified to receive it. Ah me! You can form but a faint idea of the state of things here.

May He, Who knoweth when a sparrow falleth, watch over and protect you all. Read Isaiah, 8 chap., 9 to 13 vs. inclusive.[20]

Origin of Secession
Slavery—idleness—hot bread—dyspepsia, and of course derangement of stomach and brain from this Ignorant, violent woman.
Shallow thinking, violent men—negro traders—false teaching—
false preaching—corrupt press. General Lee will do much to cure
this, plenty of work and short rations, giving a healthy tone to the
stomach, which I am not sure is not the seat of all afflictions—at
any rate it is of patriotism from the way I see things working.
Nothing truer than that.

Satan finds some mischief still for idle hands to do.

I knew the night these gentlemen set out a few Union people had
done for them what they could, but they were poorly provided for
the weather, which became intensely cold—so cold that some poor
fellows in the Confederate service froze to death, and the prisoners
on Belle Isle suffered beyond description. The man, who agreed to
go with them as guide and on whom they depended, realizing his
perilous situation, deserted them and returned in a few hours to
his home. Their safe arrival, after many days of suffering and wandering, gladdened our hearts.

*As with some other entries, Elizabeth wrote the following after the war
ended and inserted it into the 1864 portion of her journal. It was apparently written while Jefferson Davis was in prison at Fortress Monroe for
two years after his capture on May 10, 1865. He was never brought to
trial. Elizabeth wanted her readers to know the horror felt by one of the
Yankee spies faced with death.*

The public being at present not with sympathy for Jeff Davis—his
health, imprisonment and trial, it may be of interest to review and
republish an episode in his life—the death by hanging of Spencer
Deaton, taken from the *Richmond Examiner*[21] of February 20th,
1864:

Execution of a Spy

Yesterday, shortly after noon, the extreme penalty of ignominious death, for outraged military law, was visited upon
Spencer Deaton at Castle Thunder. He was arrested, tried,
condemned and hung as a Yankee spy, found inside the
Confederate lines. His execution was fixed for yesterday
week, but upon his own representation in a letter addressed
to President Davis, that he was not ready to die, he was
respited one week.

The demeanor of the condemned, since the day sen-
tence of death was passed upon him, up to the last moment,
was that of abject fear and despair.

He was sustained in the interval by immense potations
of whiskey and laudanum. The surgeon of the Castle fort,
Dr. [T. E.] Upshur, expressed the opinion that but for the
daily administration of this stimulant, he would have died
long since of mental prostration, as he rarely partook of
food, and was rapidly wasting away.

Yesterday's sun brought the day upon which Deaton's
respite expired, and no further extensions came or could
be hoped for. So the prison officials warned him, and up
to noon he was busy in his cell with his religious advisor,
preparing his soul for a transition of worlds.

At a few minutes past 12 Noon, every thing calculated
to give fatal dispatch to the machinery of death having
been arranged, Deaton, the condemned, made his
appearance at the Castle door way, which opens into the
enclosed yard, near the centre of which the scaffold was
erected.

He was accompanied by Adjutants [Thaddeus] Ward and
Wiley[22] of the Castle, and detective [John] Caphart, each
supporting him as he shuffled towards the foot of the
engine of death, and regarding it with a look of blank,
but apathetic horror.

Of tall, thin stature, ghastly face, relieved by a black moustache and infernal, long bony arms, dressed in a dilapidated frock-coat, red, dingy, homespun trousers, and tall black felt hat, such as yankee officers usually wear, the condemned was a livid picture of abject, yet speechless terror and despair in the presence of death that stupefies while it appalls.

It was cold, bitter cold, so much so that the guard, officials, and spectators admitted within the high enclosure, were almost benumbed while the short preliminaries were being gone through with. Not so Deaton; his brow was clammy with sweat, that in his mortal terror burst out all over him.

Standing beneath the gallows, Captain [Dennis] Callahan, of the prison post, read aloud the proceedings and finding of the court martial which condemned, and the death warrant which sentenced him.

Deaton listened to all, his eyes fixed in vacancy, his hands in his pockets, and his hat on his head. Rev. A. D. Dickinson, camp colporteur, then came forward and engaged with the condemned in a most fervent prayer, Deaton putting in a response now and then. At the close of the prayer, Deaton turned round and went up the ladder, with difficulty, and not without assistance. Detective Caphart followed him upon the platform and pinioned his arms. A negro adjusted the rope to the beam; the noose was fixed upon his neck, his feet tied, and the white muslin cap drawn. But Deaton's arms were so long that, though pinioned at his elbows, he reached up and removed his death cap once or twice. Deaton sank down, and stretched out the length of the rope on the top. Caphart returned to him, begged him to stand up like a man, and put him on his feet again, but he sank down again, saying, "No, I cannot stand. You must hold me up."

Adjutant Wiley then came up, and supporting Deaton,

standing on the ladder, while Caphart hastened down and drew the bolt which secured the trap, and the work was done.

There was apparently little effort at struggling. The trap fell at fifteen minutes after twelve o'clock. The body, after hanging thirty minutes, was examined by Surgeon Upshur, who pronounced life gone. A few minutes later, the guards, officials and spectators were gone, the body cut down, coffined and en route for interment.

The intensely cold weather prevented a large attendance of spectators outside the enclosure, but nevertheless, the housetops, windows and other elevations affording a view of the execution were early peopled with men, women and children. All the arrangements for the execution were carried out promptly and swiftly.

The following is an abstract from the personal history of the condemned.

Spencer Deaton belonged to Co. B, Tenth East Tennessee Renegade Infantry, Colonel Joseph E. Cooper, commander. He was apprehended on the 17th of August, 1863 by members of General Samuel Jones' command upon the charge of being a recruiting officer for the Yankee army, within our lines twelve miles from Knoxville.

He was tried by a court martial, convened in Western Virginia, on the charge of being a spy, and that charge being sufficient to convict him, he was not arraigned on the other count. Deaton was a native of Tennessee, and about thirty-six years of age. His father, William Deaton, resides at Strawberry Plains, Jefferson County, Tennessee. A brother commands a Yankee renegade regiment now operating in East Tennessee.

The longest entry in Elizabeth's journal concerns the February 28 to March 4 raid on Richmond by General Judson Kilpatrick and Colonel Ulric Dahlgren. They were attempting to free Union prisoners held at

warehouses and Belle Isle. Having precipitated the raid by her letter to
General Butler, here Elizabeth gives great detail of the event and her own
experiences, which she added to her diary later.

Every available man was called out. There was an awful quiet in
the streets; the heavy silence was oppressive. I drove out in the
afternoon and I saw all the militia drilling, among them Northerners, and some I know to be Unionists. So potent is fear to blind
conscience! At night we could hear the firing of the cannon from
ten till eleven o'clock.

The body of men under Col. Dahlgren rapidly approached the
city, when through the treachery of a guide,[23] he failed to form a
junction and cooperate with Col. [*sic*] Kilpatrick. He was forced to
deviate from his course and make his way to the peninsula. Every
effort was made to intercept him. Col. Dahlgren, however, succeeded in reaching King & Queen County after dark, when he fell
into an ambush, was fired upon and killed.

It seems that two companies of cavalry, Col. [Fitzhugh] Lee's
Rangers and King and Queen Cavalry,[24] were in the vicinity of
the Court House, but not in actual service, having been disbanded
for one month for the purpose of recruiting their horses. As soon
as the alarm was given, these, together with the King and Queen
Home Guards and [Captain John William Magruder][25] McGruder's
[*sic*] Cavalry, were either sent for or they hastened on their own
accord to join Col. McGruder, who was in command.

Steps were taken to intercept Dahlgren and men placed in
ambush at different points. It is said that upon hearing a rustling
in the bushes, Dahlgren, who was riding ahead, called to his men
to rally; that he believed the enemy was there, and so saying, fired
in the bushes. The fire was returned and Dahlgren, being struck,
fell from his horse and instantly expired.

By whom the fatal shot was fired, it is impossible to say. I have
heard of no less Man proven who claims this honor. It has been
asserted that there were five balls in his back, but reports vary—the
number from three to five. It is said that his horse whirled at the

sudden flash of the light and this caused him to be shot in the back; for those who were present admit that nothing could have been more gallant and daring than his bearing and that he led his men with his face to the foe! Some say that he was accidently [sic] killed by his own men, but the general belief was that when his horse whirled he fell by the rebel fire.

Upon the fall of Colonel Dahlgren, his men broke over a large ditch and cap and stock fence, a very strong dangerous fence to leap, and remained all night in an adjacent field, surrounded by the rebels. All this occurred in thick darkness, on a misty, cloudy night. The next morning they were forced to surrender, sixty men[26] and over [a] hundred horses being captured, about forty men succeeding in making their escape. Six or seven of them were betrayed by a negro to whom, after two days of fasting, they applied for food, which he promised to bring them, but instead of so doing, betrayed them.

The next morning a coffin was made, the body of Dahlgren placed in it and buried, where he was killed, in a slashy, muddy hole about two feet deep in the fork of two roads, one leading from Stevensville, the other from Mantua ferry.[27] After a few days it was disinterred by order of the Confederate government, brought to Richmond, and for a time lay insulted [sic] in a box car at the York River Railroad depot; it was buried, as the papers said, at 11 o'clock at night, no one knew where and no one ever should know! Shocking to decency was the talk over his corpse.

It was afterwards discovered that he had been secretly buried by order of the authorities, by Major John Wilder Atkinson, and two or three men on the spot where we buried prisoners below Oakwood Cemetery.[28]

The heart of every loyal person was stirred to its depths by the outrages committed upon his inanimate body, and to discover the hidden grave and remove his honored dust to friendly care was decided upon. Several endeavored to trace it and Mr. F. W. E. Lohmann[29] succeeded in doing so, willingly running the risk of its removal, which all knew here was perilous in no small degree.

Arrangement had been made to carry it to the residence of Mr. William S. Rowley, some short distance in the country, and accompanied by Mr. Martin M. Lipscomb,[30] on the cold, dark and rainy night of April 5th. Mr. Lohmann went to the ground and with the aid of a negro took up the coffin, opened it and identified the body by the missing limb (having lost his right leg below the knee). It was then put into a wagon and Mr. Lohmann drove it to Mr. Rowley's. Upon arriving at the farm of Mr. R., the coffin was carried into an outbuilding, a kind of seed or work shop, where Mr. R. watched the rest of the night beside it. In the morning a metallic coffin, which had been procured by Mr. Lipscomb, was brought by F. W. E. Lohmann and his brother John. A few Union friends saw the body. Sad and sorrowful were their hearts and tender wailing fell from their lips. Col. Dahlgren's hair was very short, but all that could be spared was cut off and sent to his father before Richmond fell. Gentle hands and tearful eyes[31] examined his breast to see if there was any wound there, but nothing of the kind could be perceived. The body, except the head, was in a perfect state of preservation, fair, fine and firm the flesh . . . here and there a purple spot as if mildew. This was remarkable considering the length of time of the burial, unless, as was thought, it was becoming adipocere, the ground in which he was buried being very damp. The comeliness of the young face was gone, yet the features seemed regular and there was a wonderful look, firmness or energy stamped upon them. His dress was a shirt of the coarsest kind, not even fastened; pantaloons of dark blue cloth; a fine cotton sock was on his left leg; the right leg was wanting below the knee. His right hand was carelessly thrown across his person; the left, robbed of its little finger, was resting on his left thigh. I know a gentleman who saw a man cutting away his little finger. Around the body was wrapped a blue military blanket.

The body was taken from the rough, coarse coffin, and placed in the metallic one, the lid of which was sealed on with a composition improvised by F. W. E. Lohmann, as there was no putty to be found in Richmond. This coffin was placed in Mr. Rowley's wagon, which was then filled with young peach trees packed as the nursery men pack them, the coffin, of course, being covered and concealed. The horses being attached, Mr. Rowley took the driver's seat and drove all that remained of the brave young Dahlgren through the several pickets, one of which was then the strongest around Richmond for the reason that twice before this, had the Federal forces been within the outer line of batteries, and at this very place had Dahlgren[32] fought for hours the day before his death. And if one had run his bayonet into this wagon only a few inches, death would certainly have been the award of this brave man [Rowley], and not only death, but torture to make him reveal those connected with him—his accomplices.

The forged papers said to have been found on Colonel Dahlgren's body had maddened the people, and Southern people when maddened, who have been used to giving way to wrath with violence on negroes, stop not at trifles. A slave population (defenseless) tempts a people should right offend them to be passionate and regardless of consequences. Free countries have no such scape goats as our poor slaves, and they don't understand us.

When Mr. Rowley approached this picket post he realized, for the first time, his peril. He drove up to the tent, stopped before it, and let fall the reins with the appearance of perfect indifference. The lieutenant, being present, ordered a guard to examine that wagon and passed on into the tent. It so happened that at this moment a wagon was passing into the country on the opposite side of the road, and the guard, seeing Mr. Rowley at leisure, proceeded to search this first. Coming up to Mr. R., he said, "Whose peach trees are those?," observing at the same time, "I think I have seen your face before." "Yes," replied Mr. R., "and I have yours." "Where?," asked the guard. "At your own house at ———," said Mr. R. "Ah, yes, at such and such a time," was the rejoinder, and then the friendly talk and greeting. "But, whose peach trees are those?" again inquired the guard. "They belong to a German in the country to whom I am carrying them," said Mr. R. By this time, another cart or wagon had come up and required examination, which was thoroughly done. Then the man returned and the conversation was resumed in reference to peach trees, about the lateness of the season to transplant them, etc. Another cart, then a relapse to the culture of peach trees, with cementing friendship. In this way some time passed during which quite a number of wagons were examined, this being the principal road to the city,[33] from that direction, until the lieutenant sang out from the tent, with wrath, to the man "to get through searching that wagon and let the man go on. Not to keep him there until night." The guard said, "it would be a pity to tear those trees all up, when you have them packed in there so nicely." "When I packed them," replied Mr. R., "I did not expect them to be disturbed, but as it is, I know ————." Then another wagon to be examined, and the lieutenant called to him a second time to let that man go. The guard said, but not loud enough for the lieutenant to hear, "I don't want to hinder you any longer. I think it all right, at any rate your honest face is guarantee enough for me—go on." Rowley drew up the reins and started off, greatly relieved.

The two Lohmanns,[34] who had flanked the pickets, now approached the wagon and seating themselves on each side of Mr. Rowley, directed him which way to drive. They proceeded until they came near the Yellow Tavern,[35] where General Stuart, the noted rebel cavalry officer, was killed; then, leaving the turnpike, drove west about ten miles in the country to a farm of a German named Quick.[36] There the grave was quickly dug and the coffin placed in it, and two faithful German women, one with a spade and the other with a shovel, helped to fill it. A peach tree was planted over it. The two Lohmanns then returned home in the wagon, and every true Union heart, who knew of this day's work, felt happier for having charge of this precious dust.

Where now is the paper, said to have been found upon Colonel Dahlgren's body?[37] Why was it that it was never publicly exhibited, and that so few ever in high authority had a glimpse of it, so studiously was it concealed? I know search was made for it by those who had access to the different bureaus of the war office, yet such search, though diligently prosecuted, proved unavailing.[38]

The deduction is inevitable that said paper was prepared in Richmond, to preserve a particular [belief], and, viz. to irritate and inflame the Southern people. We made capital by exhibiting General [John] Pope's coat,[39] a yankee skull, etc, and certainly no one, knowing us, would have suspected us of the false delicacy of withholding from public exhibition a paper, which if genuine, would wonderfully have subserved our ends, unless we had feared the handwriting might be detected by some of the Richmond experts and the fact made known to the world.

Does not the whole thing tell of [Secretary of War Judah] Benjamin, [Confederate Congressman Louis T.] Wigfall and, in short, the "Southern Confederacy?" If this paper were genuine, it would have been preserved as our richest treasure, and used, even now, to the prejudice of the whole North, and damning murder to the name and fame of Colonel Dahlgren.

The course, too, of the Federal authorities, since the 3rd of 1865, gives the lie direct to any claim to genuineness such document might have so far as the United States Government is concerned. The people, who could put powder under a building filled with helpless prisoners,[40] with the intention of launching them into eternity in certain contingencies, in a part of the city, too, thickly populated at the time, would scarcely scruple to manufacture mental power from the pocket of a dead prisoner to inflame their own people.

Charity, even, does not incline us to believe that the paper in question was destroyed on the 2nd and 3rd days of April 1865, when the greater portion of books, papers and other government documents were committed to the flames at the different departments, for we know that Many of the most valuable were consigned, for safe keeping, to the care of different individuals connected with the Confederate States Government, and that paper would, if genuine, have been carefully guarded and preserved, even amidst the horrors attendant upon those two memorable days.

Note: The pretended order of Dahlgren as given by the Rebel Press spelled his name wrongly, which is of course, proof present that he never signed it.

The *Whig* of March 7, 1864, in alluding to Dahlgren's said [paper], has the following:

The captured bandits.

Presuming the documents found on the body of Dahlgren to be authentic, the whole question of the recent attempt to invade Richmond, burn and sack it (with all the other horrible concomitants of such a scene) can be stated and disposed of in few words. It requires no fine disquisition to see our way clear as to what should be done with those of the bandits who have fallen into our hands.

But it does require nerve to execute palpable convictions of our judgement—a judgement which will be promptly sustained by the civilized world, including China, the most truculent of nations; nations not uncivilized.

Are these warriors? Are they soldiers, taken in the performance of duties recognized as legitimate by the loosest construction of the code of civilized warfare, who have forfeited (and expect to lose) their lives! Are they not barbarians redolent of more hellish purposes than were ever the Goth, the Hun, or Saracen! The consentaneous voice of all Christendom will shudderingly proclaim them monsters, whom no sentimental idea of humanity, no timorous views of expediency, no humbling terror of consequences, should have shielded from the quickest and the sternest death.

What more have we to dread from Yankee malice or brutality than we now know awaits us, if success attend them? Will justice meted out to these creatures stimulate either the brutality of the Yankees on the one hand, or increase their capacity and means for diabolism on the other? Both are now in fullest exercise.

If these men go unpunished according to the exceeding

magnitude of their exercises, do we not write [*sic*] the Yankees to similar, and, if possible, still more shocking efforts? If we would know what we ought to do with them, let us ask what would ere now have been their fate, if, during a war, such a body of men, with such purposes and such acts, had made an attempt on and were taken in London or Paris. The English blow fierce and brutal repoys, who disregard and exceed the just limits of war, from the Mouths of cannon; the French fusillade there. If we are less powerful, have we less pride and self respect than either of these nations? These men have put the *caput Lupinum* [wolf's head] on themselves. They are not victims; they are volunteers for remorseless death. They have rushed upon fate, and struggled in voluntary audacity with the grim monster.

Let them die, not by court martial, not as prisoners, but as *hostes humani generis* [enemies of the human race], by general order from the President, Commander-in-chief.

Will the Cabinet and President have nerve to do what lies properly before them? This is the question in all mouths. What concerns this people most now is not whether its public officers will come out of this war with brilliant European reputations. Not whether, after leading the people out of Egypt, they shall have the reputation that Moses preserved of being very meek, but they wish protection to themselves, their wives and children and their honor.

The future character of the War

The band of robbers, incendiaries and murderers, who lately came against this City to sack and burn it, and massacre the principal personages who reside here, were selected from the different corps under General Meade, and sent under chosen officers of that Army. Meade, himself, lately returned from Washington, and it was noticed that immediately on his arrival [at the winter camp of the

Army of the Potomac at Orange, Virginia], movements
were commenced which have now had their culmination
in the fiendish foray of last week. There is no doubt the
expedition was planned and its infernal character given to
it in Washington. Lincoln and his advisers were parties to
it—perhaps instigators of it. Meade was *particeps* because if
he did not, as is probable, write the orders that were found
on Dahlgren's person, he necessarily knew of them, and
handled his army so as to facilitate their execution. Those
orders were for war under the Black Flag. On the line of
their desolation march "everything that can be used by
the rebels" was to be "destroyed," and when they had
reached Richmond they were "to destroy and burn the
hateful city and not allow the rebel leader Davis and his
traitorous crew to escape;" they must be "killed."[41] This is
a mode of warfare recognized by no code nor crew of
civilization. It is war under the Black Flag. It was well
understood to be so by those engaged in it; for Dahlgren,
after offering to his men the privilege of withdrawing if
they had no stomach for the business, warned them that
if they permitted themselves to be taken prisoners they
would meet "an ignominious death." It may be very
shocking to the tender sensibilities of our authorities to
entertain the idea that this is to be the future character of
the war, but we respectfully suggest that they have no
option about it. This is a matter about which it does not
take two to make a bargain. The enemy have decided,
and their decision is controlling. We would have left out
of the war altogether if the enemy had allowed us, but
they would not. When forced into it we would have conducted it in accordance with the usages and principles of
civilized nations, but they will not have it so. We are pas-
sive and powerless in the matter, and we are simply
obliged to accept the conditions forced upon us. As war
can only be met by war, so war under the Black Flag can

only be met by war under the Black Flag. If the President
cannot recognize this fact, the army can recognize none
other.

It is very plain and very inevitable.

The two articles which follow, taken from the *Richmond Dispatch*
March 9 and 11, 1864, are given as specimens of the "interperative"
[*sic*] style, at that time freely indulged in by all city papers.

Colonel Dahlgren [March 9]

The local columns of the City papers, or of most of them
yesterday morning made reference to the interment of
the body of this dead Federal officer, and intimated that
it was intentionally so put away as not to be found any
more. This, it was inferred, was considered as well merited
disposal of the last of him. We know nothing positively on
the subject, yet since this statement has reached the public, we venture to suggest that the remains might have
been applied more profitably. The only use to which we
can practically devote the remains of the dead is to employ
them with some moral advantage to the living. We bury
with ceremony and pomp the great and the good, and
mark their resting place with a tomb of enduring material, on which we inscribe some account of their virtues for
the admiration and emulation of future generations. Why
may we not derive a beneficial lesson from a monument
of an opposite character? Suppose Dahlgren to be buried
in a prominent place, and that a stone should be set up
over it simply and briefly stating that there he was and
who he was. It would be a monument of infamy—a bea-
con to warn all of the fate of one so execrable. The youth
of Richmond when passing the spot, would derive fresh
courage and renewed determination to defend their country and their homes as they contemplated the last resting
place of the man, who led on a band that came to burn

their city and butcher her people. Don't put Dahlgren
entirely away—let his memory live and endure as long as
possible.

Dahlgren [March 11]
The miserable wretch, whose orders to hang Jeff Davis
and burn and sack the city, have brought down a storm of
deserved execrations upon his head, it ought never to be
forgotten, was no worse than the rest of his Yankee comrades in crime, and not as bad as the monstrous villains of
the Washington Cabinet, under whose express and explicit
orders he was of course acting. Kilpatrick and all the other
officers of this and every other expedition to Richmond
have no doubt had the same programme dictated by the
same supreme authority. The misfortune of Dahlgren was
that he was found out. But he was no worse than Kilpatrick and other base men, who consented to carry out
orders that none but devils could have devised. The chief
criminals are Lincoln, Seward, and the Black Republican
crew at Washington—men who have deliberately planned
and directed the commission of one of the most gigantic
crimes in the annals of human warfare. Upon them let the
execrations of all civilized men descend, as well as upon
their miserable tools, some of whom have been sent to that
great tribunal where all must one day stand and receive
the just reward of their deeds.

The *Examiner* of March 8, 1864, had several pieces in reference to
Dahlgren's expedition, a few of which are here given. They speak
for themselves.

Dahlgren's body was boxed up at Walkerton on Sunday
and brought to Richmond, with the object, we understand, of its positive identification, and the establishment
of the fact of finding of the infamous documents upon it,
all of which had been attested by witnesses. Henceforth

the name of Dahlgren is linked with eternal infamy, and
in the years to come, defenseless women and innocent
childhood [sic] will peruse, with a sense of shrinking horror,
the story of Richmond's rescue from the midnight sack
and ravage led by Dahlgren. It would seem something
of the curse he came to bestow upon others lighted upon
his own carcass, when it fell riddled by avenging Southern
bullets. Stripped, robbed of every valuable, the finger cut
off for the sake of the . . . rings that encircled them. When
the body was found by those sent to take charge of it, it
was lying in a field stark naked, with the exception of the
stockings. Some humane persons had lifted the corpse from
the pike and thrown it over into the field, to save it from
the hogs. The artificial leg worn by Dahlgren was removed,
and is now at General [Arnold Jones Elzey] Ely's [42] headquarters. It is of most beautiful design and finish.

Yesterday afternoon the body was removed from the car
that brought it to the York River railroad depot and given
to the spot of earth selected to receive it. Where that spot
is no one but those concerned in its burial know or care
to tell. It was a dog's burial, without coffin, winding sheet
or service. Friends and relatives at the North need inquire
no further; this is all they will know—he is buried a burial that befitted the mission upon which he came. He has
"swept through the City of Richmond" on a fine bier,
and "written his name" on the scroll of infamy, instead of
"on the hearts of his countrymen," never to be erased. He
"asked the blessing of Almighty God on his mission of
rapine, murder and blood, and the Almighty cursed him
instead."

Conduct of the enemy in the last raid.
The depredations of the last Yankee raiders, and the wan-
tonness of their devastation equal any thing heretofore
committed during the war. At the farm houses visited by
them in Goochland,[43] they destroyed the provisions,

hacked up the furniture and stole the table silver. Mr.
James W. Morson's house they set fire to three times, but
the flames were fortunately as often extinguished by the
house servants. They fired Mr. James A. Seddon's barn,
corn-house and stables. The barn was consumed, but the
negroes succeeded in saving the other buildings. But it
would be endless to attempt to particularize their acts of
vandalism, if, indeed, many of their deeds were not too
revolting to be recited in a Christian community. The
disgusting orgies in which they spent three hours in the
neighborhood of Dover Mills should bring the blush of
shame to the brows even of Yankee women. "Picked men,"
indeed! They must have been picked out for their low
tastes and brutal natures. It is for the future historian to
gather the separate facts and show up this affair in its true
colours.

The Yankee trail from Dover to Atlee's Station[44] is
marked by devastation as complete as their feats would
permit.

In the neighborhood of Atlee's they seized and
destroyed everything that would sustain the life of man
and beast.

*An unknown number of pages are missing after the previous entry. On the
next pages Elizabeth again writes of Dahlgren. These are her own words,
an expansion of the newspaper accounts.*

. . . no small print. An argument had been made to convey it
[Dahlgren's body] to the house of Mr. Rowley & accompanied by
Mr. Martin Libscomb[45] on the road & dark and rainy night of April
5. Mr. Lohmann went to the ground & with the aid of a negro, the
coffin *was soon placed in a wagon & then driven to,* taken out, opened
& identified by the missing limb. It was then put in the wagon &
Mr. Lohmann drove it to Mr. Rowley's. The cap he wore was found
by the Fed. soldiers in a trunk belonging to the step son of the man

who kept. . . . His cap was found at [the] K & Q tavern belonging to
the step son of the man who kept this house [tavern]. This with
other circumstances caused so much indignation on their part as the
burning of most of the buildings at this Ct. house.[46] There were
several companies which were in the vicinity of King & Q Ct.
House at this time. These were Co., in part, of Lee's Rangers,[47]
McGruder's [sic] whole Co. (120 men) & the greater part of Kg &
Queen Cav[alry] and the Home Guard, Capt. Bagby's Company,
and under the command of Col. McG. At the time of the Raid,
Lee's Rangers & Kg. & Queen Cav. were not actually in service,
but had been ord[ered] banded to recruit their horses. As soon as
the alarm was given, these men were sent for or hastened on their
own to join McGruder; were taken to intercept Dahlgren & Men
placed in ambush at different points. The rebel statement is that in
hearing a rustling in the bushes & night coming on, Dahlgren riding ahead, called to his men to rally; that he believed the Rebels
were there, and so saying, fired into the bushes. He was instantly
killed by them [the Rebels]. It is impossible to say. Some say that
there were five balls in his back. The number, though, of balls varies
from three to five. It is said the reason he was shot in his back was
that the flash of the sudden light startled his horse, who started so
sharply that the balls took effect in his back. And the rebels say he
was shot accidently [sic] by his own men, but it is generally believed
that his horse jumped. He fell by the rebel fire. Many claim the
honor of this shot. I have heard some who say they killed Dahlgren.
After Dahlgren was killed, the men [Dahlgren's men] seeing his
horse fall, broke over a large ditch & a cap & stake fence, which is
a very strong & dangerous fence to leap. They remained all night in
the Mantuapike field, surrounded by the rebels. All this occurred
in thick darkness, a misty cloudy night.

The next morning these men were forced to surrender—sixty
men & 100 horses were made prisoners. 20 men, I believe, escaped.
There were six or seven betrayed by a negro. They had been two
days in the field without food, & applying to a negro. He promised
to bring them food, instead of wh[ich] he betrayed them. The next

morn[ing] a coffin was made. Dahlgren was put in it & buried where he was, abt. two feet deep in a shallow hole at the fork of the two roads, one heading from Stevensville & the other from Mantuapike Ferry. After a few days, by order of the Confed[erate] Govt., he was disinterred, brought to Richmond—lay in a R.R. Car, & was buried, the papers said at 11 o'clock at Night. No one knew where & no one ever should know, & shocking to decency was the hostile talk over this corpse. He was secretly buried by orders of Govt., Major John Wilder Atkinson & two or three men, where we buried prisoners below Oakwood Cemetery.

The heart of every loyal person was stirred to its depths by the outrage committed upon his inanimate body and to discover the hidden grave and remove his honored dust to. . . . Friendly care was decided upon. Several endeavored to have it, and Mr. F. E. W. Lohmann succeeded in doing so, having been willing to run the risk of its removal, which all knew here was perilous in no small degree.

The discovery of this body was entirely accidental, & would not have been found had not a negro been out in the burying ground at midnight and saw them bring in Dahlgren. It was carried out during the night in a four muled Govt. wagon. One man was ahead on horse back to see if there was any one in the way observing.

The negro secreted himself behind a hill and when they left marked the spot that he might know it in the day, and marked it again the next day, not knowing who the grave contained. When search was made, the negro suspected the person in the grave may be that of Col. Dahlgren's body. . . .

So much for this famous raid. A word or two respecting that notorious Confederate raider and guerrilla Mosby shall conclude this chapter.

The next pages of the journal are missing, and Elizabeth's comments on Confederate Colonel John Singleton Mosby are lost. Two days after Dahlgren was killed, General Benjamin F. Butler sent another letter, which is inserted here for continuity.

Norfolk, March 4, 1864

My Dear Niece: Your Aunt Mary has decidedly improved in health, and will be so far helped by the spring air and warm weather as to make her quite well.

Your old acquaintance, the Quaker, called on me two or three days ago, and is quite well and very happy to have escaped so luckily a visitation of the prevailing fever in his town, of which you have heard. He is going back to the North soon. He says your sisters are all quarreling over the question whose baby is the prettiest, but I decided in favor of Emily's perhaps because it is the fattest. All are well and send love.

I should like to tell you about the negro soldiers here, but I suppose if I did they would not let the letters go through. Keep up good heart, Eliza. I hope we shall soon get through our trials, and meet in a better country where all will be peace and happiness.

                              Your affectionate Uncle, Thomas Ap. Jones

When Elizabeth applied acid and heat to the letter, the following appeared:

The boy [B.] Wardwell[48] and Quaker have arrived. Give what account you can of the rebel rams.[49] Letter about messenger received. Does messenger need money? If so, give him all he wants, and it shall be repaid. Arrests will be made. Will there be an attack in North Carolina? How many troops are there? Will Richmond be evacuated? If any thought of it, send word at once at my expense. Give all possible facts.

Butler followed with another letter on March 22.

My Dear Niece: Your last letter came duly to hand much to my gratification. I was glad to learn by it that though you are so pressed by family cares, your health and spirits are so well preserved.

Your Aunt continued to improve a little every day, but the hope of ever seeing her again in health has almost faded from me. The children are well except little Ella. She has just had a severe attack of measles, and is now in a fair way to recover. We were a good deal alarmed at first, supposing it to be small-pox, as there is some of it about Norfolk. Mrs. Harris died last Thursday night of pneumonia. She was sick only five days, and was not supposed to be in very much danger until within an hour or two of her death.

All send love, and beg you to remember how anxiously we look for your letters to tell us about our dear friends.

Your affectionate Uncle, James Ap. Jones

The secret message read:

My dear friend Cashmeyer: I want to see you as soon as possible at New Kent Court House on business of life-long importance to you and your family. If you will not or cannot meet me there, please name a place and set a time you will meet me. You must be sure and name a place that will not endanger my own personal liberty. Rest assured I have news of vast importance for you and your family.

Yours entirely, B. Wardwell. Of course you will copy this letter for the party to whom it is addressed.

On the same day, Butler sent a letter to William S. Rowley with money to help him and Elizabeth in their spy work.

My Dear Rowley: Since I received your last I have seen your brother Charles, and am desired by him to tell you of his anxiety to see you again. His age and infirmities are fast wearing him away, and his sorrow at the long separation from his old friends and his family sensibly affects his health.

You would hardly recognize him he has grown so old. His oldest boy Tom is in the Yankee Army, much to the indignation of his father.

Tazwell Taylor has left Norfolk, and gone to live in Baltimore, and I hear that Rev. Mr. Wingfield, who was set to work on the streets by Wild, but who has now taken the oath, is going to Baltimore to live.

Do you ever hear of my niece in Richmond? She writes me occasionally, but is so engrossed in matters of family interest that I rarely hear of the fate of old friends.

Give my regards to your wife and all the family. Send an [all] letters for your brother to my care and I will see that he gets them.

Very truly your friend, James Ap. Jones

The translation read:

My dear Sir: The bearer has fifty thousand (50,000) dollars for you, good Confederate money. Please see our friends and have in working order at once. Employ none only those you know to be faithful, brave and true. We wish to have your men do precisely what we wished and talked about having done before we left. Say to them if we succeed we shall be able and fully prepared to remunerate them for their services rendered.

As soon as possible we shall give you further orders.

Respectfully yours, James Ap. Jones

P.S. Please give the bearer a receipt for the amount of money received.

The journal resumes with a local newspaper's comments about Elizabeth and her mother and an explanation of "Fast Days." The latter were ordered by the Confederate government to save on the consumption of food.

Rapped over the Knucks

One of the city papers contained, Monday, a word of exhortation to certain "females of Southern residence, (and perhaps birth), but of decidedly Northern and Abolition proclivities." The creatures, those specially alluded to, are not named. "Were their names revealed to the world, it would doubtless be found that they were Yankee off shoots, who had succeededley [sic] stinginess, double dealing and cuteness in arressing [sic] out of the credulity of Virginians a good, substantial pile of the root of all evil. If such people do not wish to be exposed and dealt with as alien enemies to the country, they would do well to cut stick while they can do so with safety to their worthless carcasses." These ladies were my mother and myself—God knows it was but little we could do—Chivalry.

These stories of implying luxuries, etc. were utterly false—a little chicken soup and corn meal gruel etc.—were the proscribed delicacies [we took to the prisons] for these helpless prisoners— these sick and wounded men. And it was the giving of this necessary nutriment which caused fearful threats to these ladies.

Fast Days

From time to time we had fast days appointed by Jeff Davis and occasionally thanksgiving days. Provokingly Sabbath-like were all these occasions and more scrupulously observed than the Sabbath. The markets and stores were closed. These were considered test days of loyalty, for treason ever spoke of itself as "loyal" and "sound."

I heard a minister, soon after the commencement of the war, give notice in his church that a certain day had been set aside as a day of fasting, humiliation, etc., but that he could not see what it was for, as the South had never done any thing wrong or any thing to fast for. Now, imagine this from the pulpit! He went on to speak of the beams in the eyes of the North, and I suppose it was about as comfortable a discourse as anyone had enjoyed. For years, contrasting ourselves with these corrupt people of the North and

other lands, who had not the privilege of our Christianizing insti-
tutions—we seemed to please ourselves with the order of our own
sanctity.

We always tried to have a little better dinner than usual on fast
days, as it was a holiday. It was a great comfort to see and talk with
any fellow loyalists, if that were possible. At last we learned to look
on these days as memories of good, for they were generally followed by some Federal success. The papers used to give us a syn-
opsis of the sermons in the different Churches. I see in the *Whig* of
April 11, 64 an account of a "Fast Day in R[ichmond]." I extract an
account of a "Fast Day in Richmond."

After elating that the recommendation of Congress, that Friday, the 8th inst., should be set apart as a day of fasting, humiliation
and prayer, had been very generally observed in the city, so far as
the suspension of business and public religious exercises denoted a
compliance with the well timed recommendation, and that able,
appropriate and impressive discourses had been delivered at all the
churches, the *Whig* thus proceeds:

Preaching at the Theatre at night—
An immense Congregation
The advertisement in the morning papers that religious
services would be held at the Theatre, at night, in connection with the current report that D. Burrows, the
pastor of the First Baptist Church, would deliver a discourse on the occasion, evoked a good deal of comment
during the day. Some people refused to credit the report
that D. Burrows would preach at the Theatre, as he had
not long since denounced it as a sink of iniquity. Others
believed he possessed that degree of Moral courage which
would embolden him to appear in the very courts of
Satan, and rebuke the notaries of sin, and that, therefore,
he would not fail to preach at the Theatre, if the opportunity were offered him to do so. These and various other

opinions and conjectures were expressed, and, influenced by the novelty of the event, hundreds of persons resolved to be present.

The credit of originating the meeting at the Theatre belongs, we believe, to Rev. M. Cameron, chaplain of the Maryland line. He applied to Mr. Ogden, the Manager for the use of the building for the purpose, and it was cheerfully conceded.

Precedents for the Meeting

The first instance on record is of a disciple of Jesus entering a Theatre is that mentioned in the 19th Chapter of Acts. Demetrius, a silver smith, who made silver shrines for Diana at Ephesus, becoming alarmed at the success of Paul's preaching, called together the workmen of like occupation and harangued them. He told them not only was their craft in danger, but that the temple of the great goddess Diana would be despised and her magnificence destroyed. This caused a great uproar in the city, and the people having seized Gaius and Aristarchus, Paul's companions, made a [words missing], and would have entered in with the people, but his disciples would not allow him to do so. And certain prominent men, who were friends of Paul, sent to him the request that he should not venture into the Theatre, and it would appear that he heeded their advice.

This incident does not, of course, furnish any precedent for the meeting of Friday night at the Richmond Theatre. Whatever applicability to that event it may have, if any, the reader must discover for himself. The practice of holding religious services in Theatres is common in European countries, and it is well known that, during the great revival of '58, the Theatres in New York and other cities were occupied daily for prayer meetings. But with or without precedent, the meeting at the Theatre Friday night will be justified by all who believe that the word of God should be preached wherever the sinner may be converted.

Arrangements for the service—the rush for seats. The manager, anxious to do all that he could to meet the wishes of Chaplain Cameron and his coadjutors caused the elegant carpet used in parlor scenes, to be spread upon the front part of the stage. The platform, upon which the mimic throne is generally erected, was placed midway between the proscenium and a table with two lighted candles in candelabra placed upon the platform. Sofas and chairs constituted the remainder of the furniture. The damask curtain (not the horrid "drop" which presents a vulgar idea of "Arcadia") made up the background of the extemporized pulpit.

Before 7 o'clock the people began to assemble in front of the Theatre, and in half an hour the sidewalk and streets were thronged with ladies and gentlemen awaiting the opening of the doors. At half-past seven the doors were opened, and in ten or fifteen minutes every available seat was occupied. The crowd continued to force in, and, when it became impossible to accommodate any more, hundreds went away unable to get inside the doors. Ladies were seated in all parts of the building, even in the "third tier," from which the negroes were turned out to make room for the white people. Disreputable women were excluded. The audience embraced many respectable and pious citizens, and during the entire service the most perfect decorum was maintained. The number of persons present was nearly three thousand.

At 8 o'clock, D. Burrows, accompanied by Rev. G. W. Hicks, Chaplain at "Castle Thunder," and Rev. W. H. Williams, Post Chaplain in this city—all ministers of the Baptist denomination, appeared upon the stage, entering by the left-hand stage door.

The services were opened with prayer by D. Burrows, after which, was sung the hymn commencing—"Hasten, sinner, to be wise." The elections for the occasion had been printed on slips of paper and previously distributed among the audience. The hymn was sung with fine effort, a large number present joining in and their combined voices swelling in a grand chorus.

D. Burrows then read the first 25 verses of the 26th chapter of

Leviticus, after which the congregation united in singing "When I can read my title clear," etc. D. Burrows then proceeded to address the immense audience.

(I extract a portion of his remarks:)

> We are now upon the eve of the most important events. Such a marshalling of hosts for the coming conflict the world has never before witnessed. Our rulers—all who are in posts of responsibility—are making preparations to exert all of our power to secure victory and peace. This day has been set apart by them for the purpose of preparing those moral influences which will be most prominent in ensuring our success.
>
> If some patriotic genius could only invent some energy of war which would render our success certain—if he could gather the electricity of Heaven and hold it back until the favorable moment should arrive, and then let it fall with destructive violence upon the serried hosts of the enemy, how glad we all would be; how rejoiced by the certainty . . .

The next pages are missing, but I have included here the remainder of the above paragraph and the last four paragraphs from the Whig *of April 11, 1864.*

> . . . of a speedy peace. I have come to tell you there is a method by which we may accomplish these results, as if we could gather the lightnings and hurl their concentrated force upon the heads of our enemies—a method more sure in its results than any combination of human ingenuity could possibly be. I base this assurance on the authority of God's word.
>
> If this nation is in that frame of mind—that condition of uprightness of conduct, which secures the approval of God, there is not might enough in the combined powers

of earth or hell to interfere with our prosperity. No doubt
some will regard this as the "cant of the pulpit," as the
utterance of religious enthusiasm; but it is, nevertheless,
the teaching of God's word. I thank God there is so little
actual infidelity among us. Though many are practically
atheistical, yet, when I speak with those who are most
regardless of the commandments of God, I am met with
the respectful admission, *There is a God* who rules the
universe. A man is deemed a fool who believes that the
eye of the body could make itself, or come into existence
by chance. If the eye-glass could not manufacture itself,
how could the eye? But I will not present any argument
to prove there is a God.

This God is everywhere present ruling this universe.
He that made the eye shall He not see? God is a sovereign
who not only has the right to rule, but does reign—not
only in theory but in fact! He can do as He pleases. He
can carry out His own purposes in His own way, and we
cannot comprehend them. He can bring this world into
subjugation to Himself, and make the agency of man con-
tribute to that end. God is never thwarted. His purposes
are all fulfilled. He is rearing what may be called a "living temple," and has invited all to form a part of this holy
building, to be built on as "living stones," and He will
have the services of all. Those who refuse to form a part
of the temple, He will use as scaffolding, and when the top
stone is laid, all the useless rubbish around the Palace of
our Lord will be thrown to the flames.

The prosperity of a people depends upon their pleasing God. Is that not announced in His word? National
prosperity has as its basis national virtue. Even the heathen
nations, from Assyria to Rome, were prosperous whilst
virtue was cultivated among them; but when they surrendered themselves to vice and crime, destruction overtook
them. *Our* future prosperity and happiness as a people

depends upon the cultivation of God. If our rulers and
our people will, this day, humble themselves before God
and strive to obey his commandments, there is not power
enough among all the nations of the earth to interfere
with our happiness. Shall we not then, with humiliation
and prayer, implore His pardon of our sins, and consecrate
our hearts and lives to Him?

What will fasten upon us the chains of tyranny, and
subjugate us to the rule of those who hate us? The most
grievous of all earthly woes is to be ruled without our
consent in the interest of those who are our foes. That is
what we are threatened with—the very depth of social
and political debasement. What will bring us into this
condition? Not the power of the enemy. But what? *Our
own sins bring on us the displeasure of God!* God can bring us
to that condition. He can bring us to that depth of degra-
dation to which I have referred. How can we avert it? God
tells us that we can avert His wrath by sincere repentance,
obedience to His commands, and submission to His Son.
Now, if these be truths—and none who believe in the existence of God and His revealations [*sic*] can deny them—is
it not the duty of the people to cleanse themselves of sin?

*Following the above newspaper excerpt, Miss Van Lew included a short
paragraph on her opinion of Provost Marshal General John H. Winder.
Edward G. Higgenbotham, chief surgeon of the prisons, was often at odds
with General Winder over prison policies.*

General Winder, outside of the outside pressure, was a kind hearted
man, but easily imposed upon, & violent in his prejudices. [He]
would carry. . . . Higgenbotham wishes he would die.

*The next item in the journal is a strange drawing and warning Elizabeth
received from the "White Caps," a group that was the forerunner of the
Ku Klux Klan. The drawing had a skull and crossbones on it and said:*

"Old maid. Is your house insured? Put this in the fire and mum's the word. Yours truly, White Caps." Miss Van Lew makes no reference to the warning, but apparently ignored it and continued her spy work.

General Ulysses S. Grant began his attack in Virginia at the Wilderness on May 5 and 6 and at Spotsylvania Court House from May 7 to 20, 1864. At the same time Butler's forces were threatening Richmond from the south, and cannon fire around Drewry's Bluff could be heard in Richmond. Elizabeth's next entry describes the reaction in the city.

May 6, 1864

The excitement is great throughout the city, and many are the rumors. General Lee has telegraphed a victory, that [General Edward "Allegheny"] Johnson and [General Zebulon Baird] Vance were killed yesterday is heard too.[50] The fight commenced without our knowledge. This is the first day we have had any intimation of the fighting. I do not feel as if the Federals would get here this spring, but I know nothing. I saw Higgins[51] yesterday; from his position he should know, and he expected them. He almost told me so. It seems to me we have suffered past all excitement. Nothing elates me. I have a calm hope, but there is much heart sadness with it.

A few days since and who was only sixteen has been taken. Poor deranged ———— forced away! Every man, who puts his foot in the streets, is immediately taken up. The firing this morning in the direction of the Bluff[52] was very heavy and jarred the windows. We hear General Stuart is seriously wounded, and said to be in a dying state. From the account received on the fight on the Mechanicsville road, as nearly as I can ascertain the truth, is that our people were severely routed by the Union troops who fought under ambush, and when our people received reinforcements and sought for them, they had left. Just at dark the servants bring in a report that the Bluffs have both[53] been taken. The truth of this we shall know soon tomorrow. Some soldiers report it, but we are disposed to doubt it. One cannot imagine the gloom of this place now.

Since Monday [May 16] the atmosphere has been heavy with

the smoke of battle. The stores are all closed. We are not to be seen upon the streets. The alarm bell has sounded until to day, and now there are no more to be called by it. The burning woods,[54] we saw yesterday and the day before, the papers tell us, consumed many wounded Yankees lying there. Oh death and carnage so near!

May 14.

Awakened by the cannon. The firing has been uninterrupted all day, and so loud as to jar the windows. Much of the day passed upon the house top. Who can sit still, who can blame us? We look from the windows, from the grounds, from the house top. We consult with our negroes. We mingle our hopes, our fears, our prayers. "Uncle Nelson,[55] can you tell the Yankee guns?" "Yes Missis, them deep ones." Sometimes he encourages and sometimes discourages, and we hang on his words and listen for his faith and hope to strengthen us. Oh, the yearning for deliverance! The uncertain length of our captivity now reckoned by years. The almost apathy and despair which creeps into our hearts, as we drag our lengthened chain. But the mist has cleared from the sadness of McClellan's campaign, and we recognize God's wonderful providence and goodness in that defeat. For years, we breakfast, dine and sup our war. How lives the outside world! When I open my eyes in the morning, I say to the servant, "What news, Mary?," and my caterer never fails! Most generally our reliable news is gathered from negroes, and they certainly show wisdom, discretion and prudence which is wonderful.

Friday, May 27.

I saw Capt. ———, who has passed through so many hard fought battles, turn deadly pale when ordered to join General Lee. "I would as soon go into the crater of a volcano," said he. ——— & ——— were here in the evening—Poor young men!

We were on the eve of fearful bloodshed. There is a portentous calm—a great moving of troops. Mr. ——— of ——— county, told me that as many as fifteen thousand passed through Richmond last night, and that in the last few days Lee has received thirty thousand troops. Lee is at Ashland.[56] The firing has been uninterrupted all day, and so loud as to jar the windows. Much of the day passed upon the house top. Who can sit still; who can blame us? We look from the windows, from the ground, from the house top. We consult with our negroes. [Here Miss Van Lew repeats her conversation of May 14 with "Uncle Nelson."]

Pages are missing following the previous entry. The journal resumes chronologically in September when Elizabeth tells of an episode in which the Confederate Provost Marshal's office attempted to get a woman to testify against a "loyal family." Although she does not identify the family, it is hers.

Only the past of Southern loyalists to be written and blended! I can give no better idea of the system of espionage and treachery which prevailed than the following: A loyal family I well know, on hearing that Thomas W. Doswell was made Provost Marshal of Richmond, congratulated themselves saying, "we know him; he has visited at our house, & he no doubt will be friendly to us." Yet this man went himself to a lady whom he knew to be intimate with this family, and tried to persuade her to come forward and give her duty [testify against them]. From her own lips I learned this. This lady was sick one day when a person called and requested to see her. She sent word that she was ill. Another message then came from the visitor that he had come to see her in regard to her testimony against Mrs. ———. A pencil and paper were sent from the lady, with word that she did not know what he meant, and he wrote, please make the object of his visit known. The following now in possession of the United States Government was returned.[57]

Miss ———
Captain T. W. Doswell, Comdg. C.S. Police, requests that you will come to Commissioner [Johnson H.] Sands [*sic*] office on 11th St. between Broad & Capitol, to give testimony against Mrs. ———. You need not see any one

but Captain [Commissioner] Sands, if you feel a delicacy
in going. They wish your testimony to conclude the case
and would like to have you come as soon as you can. You
will not see Mrs. ———, nor will your name be mentioned to her.

Yours respectfully,
W. W. New,
Detective

Sept. 27, 1864

This lady was afterward taken from her home, and made to answer
such questions as they pleased to propose, but, true to friendship,
they learned nothing from her. Doswell had also other friends
of the same family brought before him and forced to testify. One
of them a clergyman of this city, the Rev. Philip B. Price, a man of
superior excellence of character, was told when he could say and
think of nothing to betray the mistress of this house, "to refresh his
memory." The whole and sole object was to obtain by persecution
the possession of their property, and imprison and badger a lady[58]
upwards of sixty years of age whose standing and character were
impeachable, and who, without some sworn lie, they dared not
molest. One who never did aught against their "dear young government," and was ever kind to their people, in whose home,
for humanity's sake, the Confederate private ever found a friend.
I shall ever remember the pale face of this dear lady, her feeble
health and occasional illness from anxiety; her dread of Castle
Thunder and Salisbury, for her arrest was constantly spoken of and
frequently reported on the street, and some never hesitated to say
she should . . .

The next page of the journal is missing. It continues with the following:

[There] was a feeling of strange bashfulness in standing thus
in prominent isolation, mixed with and almost amounting to
a source of guilt and shame. But the promise, "as the day the

strength shall be," was fulfilled. Our true hearts grew brave. Love of our country in its trials absorbed our being; enthusiasm lightened gloom. Fine patriotism principles and strengthens character. I have known the best of men feel their lives in danger from their partners in business & from their sons-in-law, who felt differently from them. Some aged parents endured much from their children who were disloyal. Ministers lived ever under a siege of terror. I was afraid even to pass the prison.[59] I have had occasion to stop near it, when I dared not look up at the windows. Have turned to speak to a friend and found a detective at my elbow. Strange faces could sometimes be seen peeping around the columns and pillars of the back portico, & I can name gentlemen, some of our oldest and best citizens, who trembled when their door bell rang, fearing arrest.

Towards the close of the war Jeff Davis was earnest to have a writ of Habeas Corpus again suspended and to be clothed with fullest power. Visitors were watched. When the cold wind would blow on the darkest & stormiest night, Union people would visit one another. With shutters closed & curtains pinned together, how have we been startled at the barking of a dog and drawn nearer together, the pallor coming over our faces & the blood rushing to our hearts, as we would perhaps be tracing on a map [General William Tecumseh] Sherman's progress and Sherman's brilliant raids, or glorying in our Federal leaders. Then to follow the innocent visitor to the door, to lower the gas as, with muffled face, they said good night & the last words often were, "Do you think I am watched?" Such was our life, such was freedom in the Confederacy. I speak what I know. The very names of freedom and liberty in connection with the Southern confederacy were a burlesque in curious accordance with our monopoly of the words chivalry & honor. The confederates of the North look and care to stay where they could speak as they pleased, and enjoy this fresh pass. Let them remember this [word unintelligible], and not presume when they speak in favor of the Confederate Government, of which they knew nothing, and from which they kept at a safe distance.

Again, pages are missing. The narrative continues with Elizabeth's interesting description of Castle Thunder's John Caphart.

Old Caphart

His age was not far from 70. His hair long & white, his beard long, heavy & grey, all stained with tobacco juice. His head deep buried in his old greasy high crowned, broad brimmed felt hat. His tall figure, his stoop, his forward shoulders, tottering giant. His profanity, his infidelity, of wh[ich] he excitingly boasted. His general antipathy. His fine speaking voice. His heavy club, an unfailing companion. His cursing every thing that was Yankee & every thing and every body that told . . . sympathy for a suffering Northern man. His often expressed wish that he might have the powers to consign every man, woman & child equally. . . . This man, striking in appearance, could be seen treading our streets. The sight of him made humanity sick & strong men to shutter as he passed. He was one of the Castle Thunder officials & detectives. His iniquity gained him the sobriquet of "Anti-Christ," as he seemed to possess no single characteristic of that good & benevolent Being. This name "Anti-Christ" was so common that one ignorant person thought it was his proper name, so one day a negro woman who had never heard him called by any other name & innocently thinking that it was right, when in company with a dark friend & wishing to display a great deal of her African politeness, said with much animation, "Good evening, Mr. Anti-Christ, how do you do this evening?"

This was the first time a negro had ever called the old fellow by this name & it was too much for his ill nature to tolerate; so up went the old club & out belched the usual oath, blow & curse coming together, blow after blow his wrath boiled over. "G—— d—— your blk Niggers that I'll Anti-Christ You!" "Oh please Mr. Anti-Christ, don't beat me; what have I done Mr. Anti-Christ?" & for awhile nothing w[ould] be heard but "Mr. Anti-Christ" blows and entreaties. The result was Mr. Anti-Christ was terribly insulted by "a Nigger" & "a Nigger" was terribly beaten by Mr. Anti-Christ. But the Negro not being advised of her mistake as to the name of the venerable detective went off wondering what made old Mr. Anti-Christ beat her so.

The old man having nothing to support himself & family upon but his sal[ary] of $75 Confed[erate] money per month, soon found himself in danger of starvation & for awhile was assisted from the purses of his brother detectives—their salaries were better than his only from the fact that their families were smaller & less required of their support. . . . This class were capable of great corruption & extortion.

Caphart was a sort of refugee from Norfolk, where he had once acted as a detective & had nothing to live upon but his monthly pay & this rapidly depreciating. From sheer exhaustion, produced by insufficient food, his strength gradually failed & he became [word unintelligible]—still the long white hair & tobacco stained beard, the greasy old broad brimmed hat, the familiar club, the large grey eyes and brazen stare of the old detective were seen at the C[our]t office, for he still lived to see others suffer & their pains were his pleasure. The night dark & rainy in mid winter of 64 and 65, the old detective left his seat at the stove of the office for the last time. That night a little stranger unfortunate in having to call him grand-father, opened his eyes upon the world. The old man was lying upon his bed, heard the wail of the newly born. Word was brought to him that he had a grandson. [He] raised himself. "Oh well, I must go up street in the morning & get him a p[ai]r of boots." He fell back upon the bed & was no more. It was his delight to recount the numerous executions at wh[ich] he had officiated, & he had enjoyed his heaven here in seeing the violent deaths of the unfortu-nate victims of law & the still more unfortunate who p[ai]d.

1865

Elizabeth begins the 1865 portion of her diary with an account of Lemuel E. Babcock[1] and an Englishman named R. W. Pool, a spy Babcock agreed to escort to Richmond. As a consequence of Babcock's arrest, Elizabeth had to change her code name "Babcock" to "Romona."[2]

Early in 1865 the regular spy[3] from the Army of the Potomac said, "I am directed to tell you that there will be an Englishman sent through the lines, whose duty it will be to oblige and bring you information to send through." My heart sank for here was another avenue of danger. The spy came again and again, bringing word that the man [the Englishman] would soon be here. He did not know his name. The last time he said he will come to [William] White. No one else must know him until I bring you word. "This," I said, "looks very hard for poor White." He then left to attend to some business. He had hardly left when White entered. We began to talk of the newcomer and of our seeing him. For my precaution, I learn from Mr. Jordan Rugfel[4] a fearful cry, of his bringing him at once to see me. I repeated the order that had been brought. White answered, "I did not understand it so. I do not know why my life is not as precious as the lives of others." I agreed with him. The spy came in whilst we were talking, and when appealed to by White, reiterated what he had said, but added that he was not responsible, only repeating orders.

Sometime within the week—Feb. 27th—I picked up the newspaper and read thrilling news of arrest and imed. [immediate] danger. The Englishman had been directed to be brought through the lines, it seems, by Mr. Babcock of Charles City County, an elderly man, a farmer and loyal to the Govt. If stopped on the way,

Babcock was to pretend that he was bringing a deserter (Confederate) to the city. If uninterrupted, the Englishman was to endeavor to get work, being a skilled machinist and Engineer, and to pass for a Southern sympathizer, favored then as one of our own people. (After a fatiguing walk, they reached the city, the Englishman learning on the route what people of the country they passed through.) On arrival Babcock bought refreshments for them both at Mr. Oyates[5] near the market, and then went with the stranger to an [sic] hotel—I think the Spotswood.[6] They both prepared for slumber, Babcock telling him he had something to attend to in the early morning, but would be back at breakfast. On awaking Babcock went out to transact his business, and soon returned. On going to his apartment, he found the Englishman gone. In a moment the truth flashed upon his mind. His terror may be imagined. He went out mechanically into Main Street and wandered down it. In a short time he felt a rude hand upon his shoulder, and was within the firm grasp of the Confederacy for Treason; led to Castle Thunder, and put within one of its dungeon cells. Poor White was in his quiet home when Reese,[7] [Samuel B.] Maccubbin's[8] partner as Detective [the next two words are blacked out by spilled ink] of terror and cruelty to all loyal people, entered and going up to him said, "I have just come from the other side and know that you are a traitor. I have papers for you," and putting a pistol to his head, [said] "tell all you know or I'll blow your brains out." "Blow away," answered White. "Tell all who are concerned in this thing," screamed Reese. White was led off to grace a cell.

The Englishman had arisen (on Babcock's leaving) the room, dressed himself, and going quickly out enquired for the Provost's office. There he gave himself up and papers from the U. S. Govt. implicating White, being directed to him. He offered to act in any way the rebel Govt. had use, he had plans for torpedoes and gun boats, the highest commendation of self—but alas! for him, the days for Torpedoes & gun boats had well nigh passed the winter of 1865. We had already disposed of some of our gun boats—by blowing them up, and this explosive furor was upon us. His advent was late in the day for his own glory. His coming upon our sinking ship was suspicious, and to Castle Thunder was he also sent, but not to a cell and solitary confinement as the others.

This Englishman was named Pole.[9] He said he was a chosen emissary of Mason and Slidell,[10] and earnest for the Confederacy. He had been a long time trying to get through the lines. He had joined a company in Washington, expecting to be sent to active service near the lines, intending to desert, but conditions [next words blacked out by spilled ink] kept for detailed [next words blacked out by spilled ink]. It seems he was afraid Babcock had gone to betray him, hence his hasty action. His regrets now were deep and vain that he had not apparently entered into the service of the U.S. Govt., and then betrayed the prisoners he was sent to. "There are eight or ten of them," he would say. "Oh, I could so easily have given them all up. What a fool I was." A paper Pole has written addressed to the Confederate Govt., on its way, was shown to me. It commenced in this manner: "When a man gives up principle, family, friends, country, everything for a cause you may know this, he is in earnest this one."

Mr. White was an Englishman by birth. He was of good height, slight build & kind earnest face. He had a market below the city. There was nothing against him, except the address of papers to him. He obtained by money his release. Poor Mr. Babcock suffered greatly in prison and feared he would be hung. His wife came to see him. Babcock & Pole were found by the U.S. Govt. prisoners in Castle Thunder.[11] Pole for awhile kept a grocery store at the corner of 18th and Main Sts., but left for England. By these arrests, attention of the Govt. being directed to one route, peril increased, but we have finished our story of Pole. A leaf from the unwritten past.

On April 2, 1865, President Jefferson Davis received a telegram from General R. E. Lee. The general informed him that the defense lines around Petersburg had broken and that Richmond should be evacuated as

previously planned. The city was in near chaos, and panic took over when
the Confederate rear guard set fire to the tobacco warehouses. The flames
quickly spread over the entire business district in a fire storm.

April 2, 1865

Towards the close of the day [Sunday], the young soldiers could be
seen on horseback or on foot bidding hurried farewells to their
friends. Some said they must go, though they wished to stay. Some
said they would remain, but bodies of troops stationed here and
there without the town, were hurried away—individual will knows
only obedience in the army.

I went to the front door of a neighbor. On the steps a woman
was sitting in speechless acquiescence. We spoke of the news. She
knew only the evacuation of the city.

"The war will end now," I said. "The young men's lives will be
saved."

"I have a son in the army about Petersburg," she replied.

I sympathized with her and assured her she might hope for his
life; that here would be an end of the terrible words, "the last man
must die," which were so often spoken and acted upon.

She replied, "It would be better, anything would be better,
than to fall under the United States Government."

It was useless to talk with her. Night came on; we could hear
the hurried leaving. Word was sent us that our house was to be
burned; some soldiers had said so.

Our wheel barrow was borrowed; plate, papers, gold, jewelry,
forced in upon us for security. The bursting shells rent the air and
lighted the darkness. Midnight passed, the door bell rang. Two fugitives came from Castle Thunder. How alarmed now were the officials there! The wicked Wiley, deadly pale and trembling in every
limb, unlocked, by order, the cell doors to make sure of the inmates.
These prisoners were secured and carried through the streets to be
hurried South. Some, availing themselves of the confusion in the
city, broke away from their keepers and, at intervals, found their way
to our dwelling, to be gladly welcomed; but with the terror yet

upon us, we were afraid to have a light in the room they were in. Some men I knew among the prisoners escaped from their guards and, though they lived in Richmond, wandered off about fifteen miles into the country, so afraid were they of arrest. One feeble man was made to walk fifty miles before escaping, but as the distance from Richmond increased, the guards relaxed their vigilance, thinking more of self preservation. One woman confined as a spy was obliged to walk thirty-two miles when she succeeded in eluding them, and in due time made her appearance at our house.

The constant explosion of shells, the blowing up of the gun boats, and of the powder magazine, seemed to jar, to shake the earth, and lend a mighty language to the scene. All nature trembled at the work of arbitrary power, the consummation of the wrongs of years. The burning bridges, the roaring flames added a wild grandeur to the scene.

Amidst all this turmoil, quietly, noiselessly, the Federal army entered the city. There were wild bursts of welcome from the negroes and many whites as they poured in. In an incredibly short space of time, as by magic, every part of the city was under the most kind and respectful of guards.[12]

The Federal soldiers, immediately on entrance, went to work to arrest the progress of the flames. Had it not been for them, the whole city would have been a map of smouldering ruins. Hundreds of houses had fallen victims to the spreading fires. The loss of public and private property was immense. Our beautiful flour mills,[13] the largest in the world and the pride of our city, were destroyed. Square after square of stores, dwelling houses and factories, warehouses, banks, hotels, bridges, all wrapped in fire, filled the sky with clouds of smoke as incense from the land for its deliverance. What a moment! Avenging wrath appeased in flames! The chains, the shackles fell from thousands of captives, and thousands of arms fell powerless to wield the Christianizing lash. Civilization advanced a century. Justice, truth, humanity were vindicated. Labor was now without manacles, honored and respected. No wonder that the walls of our houses were swaying; the heart of our city a flaming altar, as this mighty work was done. Oh, army of my country, how glorious was your welcome!

The wonderful deliverance wrought out for the negro; they feel but cannot tell you, but when eternity shall unknot the records of time, you will see written for them by the Almighty their unpenned stories, then to be read before a listening universe. Bottled are their tears on His ear.

CONCLUSION

The Union army arrived shortly after daybreak on April 3, 1865, putting out the fires and saving Richmond from total destruction. A small group of Federal soldiers under command of Colonel Ely S. Parker, an aide to General Grant, went to the Van Lew house to protect it and the family. When they arrived, they saw that the Van Lews had raised a large American flag.

Martial law was ordered by the occupying Federal forces and no one could leave or enter the city without a pass. General Butler sent a telegram from Fortress Monroe to Colonel James Allen Hardie at Richmond, asking him to issue a pass so that John Van Lew could come home. Butler also noted in his letter that Elizabeth was his secret correspondent and had furnished valuable information during the whole campaign.[1]

How effective were the spy efforts of Elizabeth and her mother? That she was a thorn in the side of the Confederate government was evident in her mention in her diary of constantly being watched by Confederate detectives. But more important was the testimony of the chief of the Union Bureau of Military Information, the Union Secret Service, General George H. Sharpe. In a letter he wrote in January 1867 to U.S. General Cyrus Ballou Comstock, General Grant's aide-de-camp, Sharpe proposed that Congress be asked to appropriate $15,000 to the Van Lews for their efforts. He also noted the many ways the family had aided the Yankee prisoners, by means of their influence as well as the use of their own funds. He credited Elizabeth with mastering "a system of correspondence in cipher by which specific information asked for by the General [Grant] was obtained."[2]

In a July 1, 1883, interview with the *New York Herald,* reprinted
July 17 by the *Richmond Dispatch,* Colonel D. B. Parker of Grant's
staff gave further details of Miss Van Lew's efforts to serve the Union.

> When General Grant had his headquarters at City Point
> we used to receive the Richmond newspapers in time for
> breakfast every morning through the kindness of Miss
> Van Lew. Of course the newspapers were very interesting,
> and to a considerable extent valuable, but other intelli-
> gence received from the same source was of much greater
> importance. Miss Van Lew had a friend—a trusty Union
> man—who was a clerk in the Adjutant-General's Depart-
> ment at Richmond, where he had access to the returns
> showing the strength of the rebel regiments, brigades,
> divisions, and corps, their movements, and where they were
> stationed. From him invaluable information found its
> way to General Grant regularly through Miss Van Lew's
> instrumentality. She also had a man in the Engineer
> Department, and he made beautifully-accurate plans
> of the rebel defenses around Richmond and Petersburg,
> which were promptly forwarded to General Grant.
>   Then Miss Van Lew got young [Erasmus] Ross, a
> nephew of Franklin Stearns,[3] the rich Unionist of Rich-
> mond, appointed to an office in Libby Prison. Ross helped
> a great many of our officers to escape from that horrible
> place, and so well did he play his part that not only was he
> not suspected by the Confederates, but most of our boys
> in the prison who did not escape considered him one of
> the most brutal of their jailers,[4] and when the end came
> would have been very glad to put an end to him. Several
> years ago I met Captain [William H. Lounsbury] Louns-
> bery [Seventy-fourth New York Infantry], who had been
> confined in Libby, and he asked me about Ross, who died
> several years ago. Lounsbery said that one afternoon Ross
> came into the prison as usual to call the roll, cursing the

d——Yankees, and as he passed him said in a low tone,
"Be in my office at 9:30 to-night." Lounsbery did not
know what to make of this, but he determined to find out
what it meant. To his surprise he had no difficulty in getting to the office past several guards. Once there he found
Ross, who gruffly said: "See here, I have concluded to try
you and see if you can do cooking. Go in there and look
around. See what you can find, and I will see to your case
after awhile." Lounsbery went into a back room, where he
found a complete Confederate uniform hanging over a
chair. He took in the situation instantly, and donned
the uniform as speedily as possible and walked back into
the office, which he found vacant, and stepped out
into the street. The guard did not stop him, and he had
walked only a few steps from the door when a black man
accosted him and asked if he desired to find the way to
Miss Van Lew's house. He replied that he did, and was
guided to her residence on Church Hill, where he was
secreted until an opportunity was found to get him out
of Richmond. He got off safely and came into our lines.

Miss Van Lew kept two or three bright, sharp colored
men on the watch near Libby prison, who were always
ready to conduct an escaped prisoner to a place of safety.
Not all of them were secreted at her house—for there
were several safe places of refuge in Richmond supported
by her means. . . .

. . . she had a farm in the country on the other side of
the James river from us and below Richmond. Every day
two of her trusty negro servants drove into Richmond
with something to sell—milk, chickens, garden-truck, etc.
These negroes wore great, strong brogans, with soles of
immense thickness, made by a Richmond shoemaker,
whose name I will not give because he is still living and
doing business in that city. Shoes were pretty scarce in the
Confederacy in those days, but Miss Van Lew's servants

had two pairs each and changed them every day. They
never wore out of Richmond in the afternoon the same
shoes they wore into the city in the morning. The soles
of these shoes were double and hollow, and in them were
carried through the lines letters, maps, plans, etc., which
were regularly delivered to General Grant at City Point
the next morning. The communication was kept up at
our end—by means of a steam-launch—on the opposite
side of the James early in the night. Before daylight [our
scout] would communicate with Miss Van Lew's messenger and return to our side of the river.

When we got the news that the Confederates were
evacuating Richmond, General Grant, who was at the
front, before Petersburg, sent back a dispatch to Colonel
Ely S. Parker, of his staff, to go into the city at once and
see that order was preserved and that all of Miss Van Lew's
wants were supplied. I accompanied him, and went immediately to Miss Van Lew's house to carry out General
Grant's orders. The house was filled with many Union
people. Among them was young Ross, who said he wanted
to keep out of sight, as some of our men who had been
prisoners in Libby had declared they would kill him on
sight. . . .

Because Elizabeth destroyed all the messages returned to her in
1866 by the War Department, the other specific information she
sent through the lines is unknown. She feared recriminations from
the Southern people if the notes became public. The existing letters of General Butler included chronologically with the diary give
additional clues as to the information she sent. A keen observer,
Elizabeth would have described the conditions in Richmond, such
as inflation and the availability of food. Through her bribery of
clerks in the war and navy departments, she likely was able to
obtain military information about troop and supply movements.
Her contact with Union officers in the Richmond prison would

have provided additional information about Confederate forces. Thomas McNiven mentioned that Elizabeth had bribed workers at the Richmond arsenal to sabotage munitions.

General Grant must have thought that Elizabeth was a valuable spy, since he appointed her as postmaster of Richmond when he was president, from 1868 to 1875. She was one of the few women appointed postmaster during the nineteenth century, according to U.S. Post Office records. When his second term as president ended, Grant recommended to the Rutherford Hayes administration that Elizabeth be reappointed Richmond postmaster, but she was not. Grant's visit to Miss Van Lew and her mother a little over a year after the war ended illustrated his respect and gratitude for her work as a Yankee spy.

That respect, however, was not shared by the Richmond people, among whom she had to live for most of the remainder of her life. To her neighbors after the war, she was the "witch." Calling her "the Union spy who aided the Federal Government more than any other woman in the Confederacy," the *Richmond Evening Journal* wrote seven and a half years after her death:

> A portrait of Miss Van Lew, painted in youth, represents her as lovely in appearance. To the younger generation, however, [the older Miss Van Lew], with sharpened features, white curls hanging unconfined about her shoulders and a twisted figure, she seemed a witch of a woman—a strange, uncanny creature, muttering and talking to herself as she walked the streets. She encouraged the little girls in the neighborhood to come into the grounds by gifts of fruit and flowers. Boys, however, were considered trespassers, the embargo being only raised in the case of a son of a vestryman of St. John's [Church], now a student at the University of Virginia.[5]

And the "witch," as described by the *Journal,* is still how some old-line Richmonders picture Elizabeth Van Lew today.

APPENDIX:
SELECTED LETTERS

The following letters are from the Van Lew Papers, Rare Books and Manuscripts Division, New York Public Library, Astor, Lenox, and Tildens Foundations, unless otherwise indicated. The first letter is General Benjamin F. Butler's request that John Van Lew, Elizabeth's brother, and the spy A. B. Holmes be given passes to return to Richmond. John Van Lew had deserted from the Confederate army. The Union army had taken Richmond on April 3, and had the Van Lews' home under its protection.

April 5, 1865
Col. [James Allen] Hardie
War Department
Dear Sir:
Mr. J. N. Van Lew and Mr. A. B. Holmes have applied to me to state my knowledge of them with a view of getting a pass to return to Richmond.

Mr. Van Lew was long known to me as a respectable merchant in Richmond. His family were [*sic*] loyal and did very many kind deeds towards Union prisoners and himself was obliged to flee from Richmond because of his loyalty. He came into my lines last summer, bringing me what information he had. His sister, Miss Eliza [*sic*] Van Lew was my secret correspondent in Richmond and furnished valuable information during the whole campaign. She is now the repository of the secret of the burial place

of Col. Dalgren [*sic*] whose remains were taken by the
Unionists of Richmond from a dishonored grave and put
in a place of safety known to her.

She is mentioned with commendation in some of my
confidential dispatches to the War Department. Mr. A. B.
Holmes is also a well known Union man of Richmond,
whose family is still there. Mr. Holmes has given shelter
to escaped prisoners and furnished them the means of
getting home. Mr. Holmes came through the lines in the
spring of last year and brought valuable information and
was employed by me in gaining information before the
movement of my cash.[1] I would earnestly recommend that
Misters Holmes and Van Lew have passes to Richmond,
as a partial tribute to their services.

> Respectfully,
> Benj. Butler
> Maj. Gen.

*Having spent her inheritance on her espionage efforts for the Union army
and to aid Union prisoners in Richmond during the war, Elizabeth was
broke when the conflict ended. General Grant had authorized a $2,000
payment at the war's end to reimburse the Van Lew family for their espionage expenditures, but that money did not last beyond 1867. In addition,
her brother's efforts to reestablish the family's hardware business after the
war failed. Hearing of their plight, former Union General George H.
Sharpe, who headed the Union Secret Service during the war, tried to
drum up support to request Congress to appropriate $15,000 to aid Eliza-
beth and her mother and brother.*

Kingston, Ulster County, N.Y.
January 1867
General C. B. Comstock
Head Quarters, Armies of the U.S.
My dear General
When I saw you last in Washington, we conferred upon
a matter, heretofore spoken of, and for sundry reasons

delayed, which it was understood between us was to be put on paper by myself, and would then be presented by you to the consideration of General Grant.

I refer to the case of the Van Lews of Richmond. During my visit to that city in the past summer, I became possessed of the facts of many of which I had some knowledge before which tend to show that they have a very strong claim upon the assistance of the Government. The family consists of Mrs. Van Lew, a widow, her daughter Miss Elizabeth Van Lew, and a son, Mr. John C. [sic] Van Lew, with his little children. They reside on Church Hill in Richmond, and before the war were accounted among the most substantial people of that city, having been left by Mr. Van Lew, the father, many years since deceased, in the enjoyment of a handsome patrimony.

The son, Mr. J. C. [sic] Van Lew, was a well known hardware merchant of high character.

From the beginning, the family, with all its influences, took a strong position against the rebel movement, and never ceased fighting it until our armies entered Richmond. Their position, character and charities gave them a commanding influence over many families of plain people, who were decided and encouraged by them to remain true to the flag and were subsequently able during the war to receive our agents—to assist our prisoners—to conceal those who escaped and to convey information to our armies.

By her talents and enthusiasm Miss Elizabeth L. Van Lew became the leader of the little union party in Richmond, and indeed in Virginia. By her attractive manners and free use of money she soon gained control of the rebel prisons, and our officers and men felt the effects of her care. Regular reports were taken to her of the conditions of our prisoners, and for all and each according to his necessities, she obtained indulgences; for one additional food, for others raiment and bedding, for some a few hours a week more in the fresh air, and for others escape and protection to our lines.

She influenced rebel surgeons to send our men to the hospitals, and when she got them in the hospitals, she alone went from cot to cot where lay a sufferer in blue, while all the other women of Richmond attended the men in gray. In these visits she was attended by her colored servants having beautifully laden baskets, whose contents have been the means of returning many a man to his northern home.

For a long, long time, she represented all that was left of the power of the U.S. Government in the city of Richmond. John Minor Botts wrote from prison for her advice and protection and Franklin Sterns took her orders.

Not only clothing and bedding but even furniture was sent in to prisoners, and I was informed in Richmond by the plain union people that the Van Lews marketed as regularly for Libby Prison, as they did for their own house. They put their hands on whatever of their patrimony they could realize and expended it in what was substantially the service of the U.S. Government. When their convertible property, or a good portion of it, was gone, they used in the same way the receipts of the brother's hardware store, until he (having steadily refused to bear arms even for local defense) was seized and put in the ranks, when he immediately made his way to our lines near Cold Harbor in 1864 with valuable information. This of course closed his store and nearly took away the means of subsistence of this family. But still the charities went on. The mother and daughter raised money in one way and another. They sent emissaries to our lines; when no one else could for the moment be found, they sent their own servants. They employed counsel for union people on trial—they had clerks in the rebel war and navy departments in their confidences; and soon after our arrival at City Point, Miss Van Lew mastered a system of correspondence in cipher[2] by which specific information asked for by the General was obtained.

As near as I can learn without going to the family, reference can be made to the following persons to sustain my statements. Col. S. M. Bowman of Wilkesbarre [*sic*], Penn., and Captain Chase, who was there with him, know of the care of prisoners early in the war. So also do Col. Cogswell of the N.Y. Tammany regiment, Capt. R. T. Shillinglaw of the 79th (Highlanders) N.Y. S. M., Captain H. McQuade, 38th N.Y. Vols., and Hon. Alfred Ely, from N.Y. who ought, I am told, to know all about it.[3]

Major General [J. R.] Ricketts and wife can perhaps furnish considerable testimony, and I think there is a clerk in the Treasury Department, or in a branch of it in Winder's building named Edward Taylor, who is conversant with many of the facts.

I enclose a letter from General [William Raymond] Lee of Massachusetts, who is known to General E. D. Townsend, prepared some time since with a view of a public claim being made for the benefit of the Van Lews. Such a claim before Congress, would perhaps necessitate the removal of the family from Richmond, and the virtual abandonment of their remaining property there, which they now hope to save.

I have understood and believe that Col. Streight and party owed their escape to the Van Lews, and I think that Captain Boutwell[4] formerly of the U.S. Navy, was kept in their house several months after his discharge from prison; while in defiance of the rebel government Mr. Calvin Huson was taken from prison to their home, died there, and his funeral was from their house. Col. J. Harris Hooper[5] of Massachusetts is, I think, well known in Washington and can give evidence on many points referred to herein.

For the military information readily conveyed by Miss Van Lew to our officers, I refer to Major General Butler,

who ought to be able to speak largely concerning it; while
General Grant, General [John Aaron] Rawlins, General
[Marsena Rudolph] Patrick[6] (the last named particularly)
and other officers serving at Headquarters during the
winter of 1864 & 5 are more or less acquainted with
the regular information obtained by our Bureau from the
City of Richmond, the greater proportion of which [is]
in its collection, and in a good measure in its transmission
we owed to the intelligence and devotion of Miss E. L.
Van Lew.

In addition to what is said above, I have sufficient evidence to show that a valuable library belonging to the Van
Lews was strewn broadcast through Libby prison, and that
the cash amounts furnished to Union prisoners in place of
other assistance would amount to a large sum.

The expenditures of the family during the war have
greatly reduced their means; the balance of which do not
now, I am told, produce any income of importance. The
brother is endeavoring to reestablish his hardware business,
but this of course must come gradually.

After the occupation of Richmond, General Grant
directed the sum of two thousand dollars to be paid to
Miss Van Lew on a presentation of the case by Colonel
[Theodore S.] Bowers[7] and myself, "as a partial reim-
bursement to her or her brother from whose store the
funds came." This language I find in my letter to General
Patrick of May 31st, 1865, covering the order given me by
Colonel Bowers, and which was made on General Patrick's
formal recommendation.

If it be not inappropriate, I respectfully recommend
that an enquiry be made into the facts herein stated, some
of which are on my own knowledge, and all of which I
believe to be true.

A reference to General Butler may open up more
information on many of the points, while Mr. [Charles S.]

Palmer, Mr. [Robert] Dudley, Mr. [Horace] Kent[8] and other
union gentlemen of like standing in Richmond ought to
be able to ensure accurate replies to any enquiries made.

In our last interview, you told me that I ought to name
some sum, and altho' I am afraid of doing injustice in
complying therewith, and hope that thro' the representa-
tions of other parties the sum may be made much larger,
I feel bound to recommend from a very considerable
knowledge of the matter that the sum of fifteen thousand
dollars be paid to Miss Elizabeth L. Van Lew for valuable
information and services rendered to the U.S. Government during the war.

I do this now without waiting for a future reference,
because I am just leaving home to be absent some little
time; and now, General, leaving with you, what I believe
to be the most meritorious case I have known during
the war.

I am with respect & esteem your obedient servant,

George H. Sharpe

P. S. I ought to state that the order referred to was carried
out by Captain H. P. Clinson, acting Post Q. M. in Richmond after I left, who, if I am correctly informed, is in
business in Richmond as a member of the tobacco firm
of D. C. Mayo & Co.

*Not receiving the stipend Sharpe had asked for her, Elizabeth began
seeking compensation from the U.S. government on her own. She wrote
General Butler in the spring of 1867 to ask for a meeting. Although
that letter no longer exists, Butler's answer from Boston May 14, 1867,
does, and it is included in the Van Lew Papers at the Virginia Historical
Society.*

Dear Miss Van Lew:

There is no lady in the Country whom I [would] rather
would meet than yourself. I retain a lively sense of your

patriotism and fidelity to the Country in her darkest
hours. I shall not be in Washington until about 15 days
when it will give me great pleasure to serve you if in my
power.

Yours truly,
Benj. F. Butler

*Two years later Elizabeth received compensation in the form of an
appointment by President Ulysses S. Grant as postmaster of Richmond for
four years. Grant renewed the appointment for another four years during
his second term. In the following confusing letter, Miss Van Lew thanked
Grant for the appointment, and asked him to find a position for her
brother, John Newton Van Lew. The latter was given the post of superin-
tendent of the registered letter department in the Richmond Post Office.*

April 6, 1869
Gen. U.S. Grant
Pres. of the U.S.
My Dear Genl.:
I write to you not as the president, but as a dear friend.
How I thank you for the position you have given me. God
only knows for your faith & trust in me, I thank you and
will try & prove worthy. I am not responsible for the many
things the papers say of me, and I am not responsible [for]
things which I sometimes hear I have said, but never heard
of until I am surprised by their coming to me. I do not
think you would wish to humiliate my only sensible &
beloved brother by overlooking him. I earnestly entreat you
will find him a position which will enable him to make
his living, something which our community has refused
to permit him to do. He is an [sic] sincere and faithful
Republican. And if he obtains the position he deserves,
[he] will be enabled to [run] his permits office faithful[ly]
and honest[ly]. Virginians who will be the men to support
your measures and administration, but who will never
otherwise heard of, having suffered all things for loyalty

and who would die for a principle. I have but a moment
to close for the mail. I leave my brother in your hand
& with full heart that you will do what you can for him
and me.

Respectfully, Affectionately & faithfully, Yours,
E. L. Van Lew

Six months later Elizabeth again wrote Grant, this time a letter of intro-
duction for William S. Rowley, one of the Richmond loyalists who had
been employed by General Butler.

Genl. U. S. Grant
Pres. of the U. S. of America
Dear General:
It gives me pleasure to introduce to you the bearer of
this—Mr. William S. Rowley, the bravest of the brave, and
truest of the true. At his house have I seen spies secreted,
and deserters harbored with Mr. Rowley. You will find
him a character. He is ready and willing for the most daring service was he ever formed—even to periling his own
family. The body of poor Col. Dahlgren was carried to his
house, watched over by him, and by him—alone—driven
through our strongest pickets to a friendly grave. I hope
you may be able to talk [to] Mr. Rowley—you will find
him a character. He is a man of rare principles and wonderful intuition, understood here both Mr. Lincoln and
yourself long before other people did. [Wrote] Mr. [John
Minor] Botts hoping he would commend him to you as
a person to be honored by all loyal people. Pardon my
writing so much my subject must be my apology. I think
it will gratify you to know him.

I am with great respect—
Truly Yours,
E. L. Van Lew
Richmond Oct. 2, 1869

At the end of Grant's term as president, he wrote the following letter of recommendation on her behalf when she sought reappointment as Richmond postmaster:

> Miss Van Lew was appointed by me Postmaster of Richmond, Va. soon after my entrance upon the duties of President from a knowledge of her entire loyalty during the rebellion, and her services to the cause. She has filled the office [of postmaster] with capacity and fidelity and is very deserving of continued confidence by a Republican Administration.
>
> U. S. Grant
>
> Feb. 26, 1877

In a hysterical letter written to President Rutherford B. Hayes's secretary, William K. Rogers, Elizabeth asked for help in being reappointed Richmond postmaster and claimed there was a conspiracy to get rid of her.

> Richmond, April 10, 1877
> Dear Mr. Rogers—
> You were so kind as to tell me to write you. I have wished to, but did not because I saw the fact that you were over-taxed. I speak to you now and the President. I ask, may it please you. I am hounded down. I am "hounded down." The good Lord only knows how bitterly. On account, solely on account of my principles & having stood firmly—but quietly by them. There is a terrible conspiracy on my office. This I am forced by my present situation to put up with—my chief clks are the leaders. As I am obliged to submit, it lessens the respect of the others for me—and spreads—this conspiracy has fed the outside public.
>   It cruelly undermines me all the while—It says is not so—that I have now the office my asst. P.M. works my place. I have been considerate and kind, too kind, & always

polite to all clerks. G. Mills—a man of small mental cali-
bre & pretensions—wishes my place. He is supported by
the same people from the North who are clamoring for
any office—trying to decry me. They say I am sick & cross,
peculiar, irritable old maid—and stingy. God bless the fine
men of the North. I love them—the true men—for the
blessings they would give us—but I do most solemnly
assure you, you can have no conception of the class called
carpet baggers seeking whom they may deem as redeem-
ing workers for office. I assure you all foes work in the
dark from me.

There are other gentlemen here—[U.S. District] Judge
[Robert W.] Hughes and Genl. [William Carter] Wickham
for example—who say all this clamor would stop if I had
my reappointment. I am a woman and not able to protect
myself. For that reason, I earnestly beg the President to
give me my reappointment. Does he think I am too rude[?]
I have to be so. Cruelly tortured and tried. It is terrible to
undergo crucifixion daily.

I have no time to rewrite this. I hold you in most grateful remembrance with compliments to Pres. & Mrs. Hayes.

I am faithfully & respectfully,
E. L. Van Lew

*Eight days after Elizabeth wrote Rogers, P. T. Atkinson, a former Confed-
erate soldier she had come to know as a customer, wrote President Hayes
on her behalf to ask for her reappointment as Richmond's postmaster. His
letter is included in the Van Lew Papers at the Virginia Historical Society.*

Richmond, Va. April 18, 1877
Hon. R. B. Hayes, President
Sir:
As a spectator over the great Struggle for the Richmond
post office & observing by the daily papers the great
annoyance given you by the candidates and their friends,

I feel that if I could relieve you by any suggestions of
mine how gladly would I do so, but I am a Stranger to
you personally, and any suggestions that I may make
would of course be absurd & probably too officious of
me. I am an ex-soldier of the late rebel army, but no less a
loyal citizen to my country. Miss Van Lew, one of the candidates for reappointment & the present incumbent, I
have known for many years. She stood deservedly high
with the people of this city until the breaking out of the
late fratricidal war, during which she manifested strong
Union sentiments & being so zealous a friend of the
Constitution of her Country that she gave free expression
of her sentiments and by her own volition sought the fur-
therance of that cause against which, I with equal faith &
earnestness had opposed. She was true to her country, her
whole Country. I was false to the Union but true to
my State. She has been rewarded. She deserved it. Again
reward her by reappointment. She is a good officer to all
but the prejudiced, & should not be cast off. These are
the reflections of a life long democrat who has past [*sic*]
the median of life, loves his country, with all his soul, with
all his strength, & our new Present Course we are rapidly
falling in love with. Excuse this privilege in writing
to you for though I voted against you, you are now My
president & May God protect your excellent servt.

P. T. Atkinson

*Elizabeth followed her letter to Rogers with an incomplete, rambling one to
a Mr. Howland. George W. Howland was a former member of the Third
Massachusetts Cavalry. Elizabeth complains about her discharge from her
position and relates its effect on her. She was succeeded as postmaster by
William W. Forbes, a delegate from Buckingham County to the Virginia
legislature from 1848 to 1851 and a member of the 1861 Virginia Secession
Convention. Forbes served as postmaster from 1877 to 1880.*

Richmond, June 16, 1877

Dear Mr. Howland—

You were no doubt surprised at my letter asking you to
come on here. The good Lord only knows the most bitter
persecution I have endured. I have never in my whole
life including domestic afflictions which are a life sorrow,
suffered as I have & been persecuted as I have since the
fourth of March & this has been sustained too by the Govt.
The war was nothing to it. I asked for the protection of
the President on the 10th of April. On the 19th of May I
was removed from office by the appointment of a Confederate Col. of loose character. I believe I am to be continued in office until July 1st. My health has received a blow
from which I am afraid I shall never recover. I was exceedingly anxious that some person of standing and character
should see me in the office & see my management.

I would have been glad to have seen you. I wrote you
letter after letter & all too nervous to send. I also wrote
several letters to Mr. ———, thanking him for his kindness, but was never able to send them for the same reason.
I am low now, too nervous to write, but I do not want
any one here to know this. The effort to keep up the pace
of the tremendous odds I had against me—slander[ed] &
ridiculed daily in the press & in the community in
which . . .

*Two years later Elizabeth was still writing friends and past and current
government officials, trying to get her postmaster job back. In the following
incomplete letter to an unnamed general, probably Grant, she wrote that
she was reduced to little money and food and asked him to use his influence with the newly elected president, James A. Garfield, to secure her
reappointment as Richmond postmaster.*

*She may not have actually mailed this or the previous letter for, as she
indicated above, she wrote others she did not mail. Further, no responses*

from either are with her papers, although she was careful to keep answers to her letters in other cases.

Richmond, abt. Feb. 1, 1881
Dear General ———

I beg earnestly that you will read what I write. I am in so much trouble that I scarcely know how to make my situation known to you. The utter inability I have labored under to dispose of my valuable but unproductive real estate has reduced me to great disaster, absolute need.

I tell you truly and solemnly that I have suffered for necessary food. I have not one cent in the world. I could particularize painfully to bore you & myself of the strait to which I have been reduced. I believe you will have influence with Mr. Garfield & hope that Mr. G. remembers me myself as an earnest laborer. I have a letter from him in reply to a letter I wrote to invite him to visit Richmond and stay with us & speak at a Republican meeting in 1876, w[hic]h I value myself. The letter I wrote & w[hic]h you told me you kindly left in the hands of Mr. Hayes subjected me to persecution incredible in bitterness. Some of the most uncalled for, unwarranted and malicious & bitter persecution I have endured came from my own party as you yourself have known & suffered, so have I. . . . some offices have been in the interest of certain aspirants. . . . A certain ring of their class is ruling here & strengthened lately. I do not care to write more fully. I desire a good office. I would be glad to be Postmaster, because I understand that business. Please pardon me for saying it but the mail service came in as defective. I had letter cl[erk]s who were experts at figures, letter cl[erk]s that I could have become—others who understood the rules of the office, mailing cl[erk]s conversant with mail routes, carriers who were better walkers & so of all

the routine business of the office, even to the working of
splitters. Yet as a whole there was not one single one of
them who c[oul]d run the office as well as I could giving
proper care, place and duties to all. As regarded the general supervision and needs of the office, it seemed to me
I can pretended [*sic*] it better than any of them can. [You]
may call it h[ar]d [next two words unintelligible] ability if
you please for I suppose that was what I had and what the
citizens gave and give me credit for. The present incumbent, Dr. [George K.] Gilmer[9] is not yet confirmed. Dr.
Gilmer is in debt to Mr. [Franklin] Stearns. Dr. Gilmer is
a good & honest man, but he is a Dr. and editor and has a
vineyard. He came from another section of the state, has
different ways of gaining a livelihood, & all Govt. offices
are open to men. I am a woman and what is there open
for a woman to do? I was born here. I have stood the brunt
alone of a persecution that I believe no other person in
the country has endured who has not been precluded. I
honestly think the Govt. should see that I was sustained if
any one simple and cordial is here. I was always tolerant of
difference of opinion and never discourteous. Being [so]
only makes hate. The very same social ostracism continues.
A mortgage upon my property. Mr. [John L.] Grubbs[10]
tells me he cannot get money on it as if owned by others
on account of political feeling—says this is a fact.

*Elizabeth made a trip to Washington in February and March 1881, in
an attempt to see President Garfield, but was denied an interview. The*
Washington Evening Star *condemned her editorially on March 25, and
she responded the next day with the following letter:*

The purpose of my visit was to see the President. I was
never permitted an interview, hence my repeated visits. I
thought I had won a right in times of paid to country and

recognition there. The war which marched many loyalists north impovished our family. Only the most absolute need from the great depression of my city caused me to ask for the Richmond Post Office & with my record, I believe if the question was left to the nation, it would have been decided in my favor.

Respectfully,
Elizabeth L. Van Lew
Richmond, Virginia

Elizabeth's efforts to be reappointed postmaster of Richmond failed, and instead, she was given a position as a clerk in the Washington Post Office. Six months after the July 26, 1885, death of "my friend" Ulysses S. Grant, she wrote another letter to an unnamed newspaper complaining about being labeled a spy by the newspaper. She repeated an account of her work for the Union during the war. She also told of the 1864 incident with General John H. Winder's chief detective, Phillip Cashmeyer, and how she had been held in scorn by the people of Richmond since the war. Portions of the letter follow:

I remember once going to Genl. Winder's office accompanied by my brother with a letter from Gen. Butler to Cashmeyer of Baltimore, Genl. Winder's head detective, asking him to come through the lines to communicate with him under promises etc. I took the letter from my bosom & handed it to Cashmeyer. As he read it, he turned deadly pale & was near fainting apparently. However, he recovered himself and following us out, begged me to be prudent & never to come again, saying he would come to see me. Cashmeyer has since the war brought friends of his to see me and said when he told people what I had done, they w[oul]d not believe him. Can you realize reader the danger[?] I knew Cashmeyer might betray me, though I had conversations with him and his trials and tribulations here had shown his loyalty. . . .

[I am] held in contempt & scorn by the narrow minded
men and women of my city for my loyalty. Socially living
as utterly alone in the city of my birth, as if I spoke a different language, often reminded of travelling in Germany
& not understanding the language. . . . I said to a gentlemen yesterday, a lawyer who asked me to visit his sister,
that I did not visit etc.

*Two years later, Elizabeth wrote an account to an unnamed person telling
why she left the Washington Post Office.*

On the afternoon of June 30, 1887 at just at 2 o'clk. as
I was ab[ou]t leaving the Pos[t office], the messenger
handed me a paper enclosed in a long envelope, an official
notice informing me that my pay had been reduced from
$1200 per annimum [*sic*] to $720, and that I had been
transferred to the Dead Letter office. It commenced that
P. M. Genl. [Post Master General John Milton] Niles had
[ordered it]. Miss Best, who knew that I was a good
cl[er]k, entered the room. I showed it [to her]. . . . I went
to the house of a friend, J. S. Smith, Esq. He felt indig-
nant & said if he were in my place, he would resign and
not accept their insult. I walked mechanically to my
room. The next day I gave up the rooms, for I had two,
sent back the piano & as I had had 8 days leave, asked for
the rest of the vacation to which I was entitled. This I
obtained and it giving me 22 office days, I came to my
home in Richmond. . . .

*The next letter, now at the Virginia Historical Society, was written on July
11, 1887, to an unknown person or persons. In it, she pleads for the return
of an envelope containing four slips of paper on which she had written the
names of dead Union prisoners. The "gentlemen" to whom she writes may
have been publishers interested in printing her journal and papers; perhaps
Mr. Brace was T. K. Brace, a New York publisher during and after the*

Civil War. Elizabeth indicated she had shown parts of her journal to a Mr. Brace. He would have had to have seen the journal or been told what was in it in order to know that she wrote in it of her parents, as indicated in the following letter.

> Gentlemen—
> I desire earnestly to ask you two things. You have an envelope with four slips of paper in it, on which are written the names of dead prisoners. Please, I beseech you, make no use of it. The people here feel more kindly now to me & this would enrage them, and it would be dreadful for me. Then please do not mention Mr. Ruth[11]— that slip of communicating etc—Oh! Mr Brace wrote. *I desire Mr. Brace to know that I objected to writing of myself and parentage because I thought it in coarse taste.* Of my parents I can only feel pride. I say this because I am afraid he might have misunderstood me. I had hoped for a line today. I cannot believe that you have gone over to the enemy. I do [ask you to return the envelope] with an exhibition of [the diary recounting] the work I did before honest people.
>
> Gentlemen, I am
Yrs. very truly,
E. L. Van Lew
>
> Monday—July 11, 1887
> Only say of us that we were loyal—of me. . . .

In one of Elizabeth's final letters, she writes one of the Massachusetts friends, John H. Forbes, a former Union soldier in the Fortieth New York who helped her financially in her later years. These excerpts tell of trying to sell her house and of her treatment by the people of Richmond.

> Richmond, March 20, 1891
> About two weeks ago I rec[eive]d a letter from one of my real est[ate] agts. . . . [I] only wish I could get this elephant off my shoulders. It is crushing & cruci-fying. . . .

No one will walk with us on the street. No one will go with us any where—and it becomes worse and worse, as those friends I had go. . . . Northerners coming here will be welcome. . . . We are held so utterly as outcasts here. Social outcasts. I mean that we both[12] shrink from every thing like a gathering of my fellow beings, church, concerts, lectures, every thing. No one will be seen with us any where. The good Lord—our Heavenly Father— knows it is an awful way to live. There are two or three families, of course, I can see, but two of them are Northern, and our going, I feel, is not desirable for usual reasons. The fearful effect upon my life and health of such a life you cannot conceive. Yet I know that I am respected. That is in necessity and may go with hate. Several of our first gentlemen have told me lately that I should not stay here. . . . Dear good Dr. McGuire[13] lately told me the people would never forgive me, and recommended me to go. He is my friend. Every day I think of y[ou]r mother or some of my dear, dear Boston [friends]. May God bless you all. How I wish I could live among such people. I think I shall sell this elephant soon. . . .

"We can never forget it nor ever forgive you," said a gentleman to me within the past week, & yet he is friendly to us. . . . In the two houses opposite us, two Episcopal ministers, both northern men, they will not visit here even to return calls. . . .

I could write a story with the moral—excuse its elegance—

Be true to your section and let your country go to the devil.

Oh, Mr. Forbes, you do not know my troubles—I have thought of you and your wife a thousand times. . . .

The letter to Forbes was followed by an undated letter to an unnamed person, perhaps Forbes. In it Elizabeth complains of being verbally and, perhaps physically, abused by her niece. She does not name the niece, but Elizabeth Louise Klapp, the daughter of Elizabeth's sister, Anna, was living with her at the time. Elizabeth Louise Klapp was forty-eight years old at the time of the previous letter to Forbes. Miss Van Lew was seventy-three.

> Do not think you are forgotten because you do not hear from me. I think of you and grieve to see you, but I do not care to grieve you with my sorrows. They almost kill me, break my heart—literally and truly. I live here in the most perfect isolation with my niece. We have no friendly visits, except that once or twice a year two families call. You know the women have never forgiven me. Our house is large, but our living rooms are in one end. I have told you of my niece's mania for cleaning—doing the most drudged work. This she keeps up persistently. Any inter-ference makes her beside herself, both in language and actions. God help me! What shall & what can I do! To make every one believe that she is treated dreadfully by me, that I am perpetually scolding her, and tell [sic] how dreadfully, how unkindly, she is treated. She frequently threatens me that she will raise the community against me. Many a day I go out and wander from one place to another, driven or ordered out of the house. For protec-tion, abt. two months ago, I persuaded a lady to stay with us at night for my protection. She was driven away her-self—twice—but determined to stand it, and my situation became better. She knows the truth, but she, only a week ago, was called from the city permanently. We are now entirely alone. My niece has been for the past week remarkable sensible & behaved well, but to night I have had the full benefit of such talk and abuse as hardly ever falls to mortal lot. She kept her hands off & has now left the room. There is old gen . . .

The remaining pages of the letter are missing. A fighter to the end, Eliza-
beth wrote her last letter to John K. Childrey, the treasurer of Richmond.
This note is housed in the New York Public Library archive collection.

Richmond, Va. Nov. 28, 1892
I do hereby present my solemn protest against the right
of any Easement, either state or municiple [*sic*], to collect
taxes or rather to levy taxes, without representation & ask
that this protest be recorded and published.

E. L. Van Lew

Elizabeth passed away eight years later, on September 25, 1900. Six
months later, Edmund J. Carpenter of Boston contacted the U.S. War
Department and inquired about the espionage notes she had sent through
the Confederate lines during the war. He received this reply:

March 21, 1901
. . . All papers in this Department relating to Mrs. [*sic*] Van
Lew were taken from the files December 12, 1866, and
given to her.

Five days later a similar letter was sent to John P. Reynolds, Jr., executor of
Elizabeth's estate.

In the communication from this office of the 21st instant,
it should have been added that the papers taken from the
files December 12, 1866, and given to Miss Elizabeth Van
Lew related to a request filed in 1866 for additional compensation for her services. The records show that on October 31, 1866, George B. Newton, acting commissioner of
agriculture, referred to this Department a letter from one
Benjamin Totham relating to the circumstances of Miss
Van Lew and her mother and asking that the Government
render them pecuniary assistance in view of their loyalty

and services rendered to the Government. The letter was referred by the War Department about November 15 to the agent of the Bureau of Refugees, Freedmen and Abandoned Lands at Richmond, Va., for investigation, from which it was received back about November 23 and given to Miss Van Lew on the date stated.

It is proper to add that a letter from Miss Van Lew to General B. F. Butler dated January 30, 1864, said to have been received by him in cipher, is printed on page 520, Volume XXXIII, Series I, Official Records of the Union and Confederate Armies.

No other communication from Miss Van Lew, written in cipher or otherwise, has been identified among the records of this Department, nor has the key to any cipher used by her been found.

NOTES

INTRODUCTION

1. D. R. Anderson, ed., "Biographies of John Minor Botts . . . ," 30–37.
2. John Blakeless, "Lincoln's Private Eye," *Civil War Times Illustrated,* October 1974, 22–30.
3. Dr. Robert S. Holzman, "The Soldier with Two Sexes," *Civil War Times Illustrated,* January 1975, 12–44.
4. Elizabeth Van Lew, "Occasional Journal," n.p.
5. Ibid., 472.
6. Malvern Hill Omohundro, *The Omohundro Genealogical Record. The Omohundros and Allied Families in America,* 649–51.
7. Jack G. Zehmer and Marguerite Crumley, *Church Hill,* 59.
8. Ibid.
9. "Occasional Journal," n.p.
10. Van Lew Papers, Virginia State Library and Archives, Mrs. Eliza Van Lew's April 2, 1838, letter to Charles J. Richards.
11. Ibid., John Van Lew's February 13, 1840, letter to Richards.
12. *Richmond Enquirer,* September 15, 1843.
13. Henrico County Will Book No. 11, 266–73.
14. Zehmer and Crumley, 59.
15. John Albee, "Elizabeth Van Lew Papers," Swem Library, College of William and Mary, n.p.
16. Fredrika Bremer, *The Homes of the New World: Impressions of America,* 509–11.
17. Ibid.
18. Van Lew Papers, Virginia State Library and Archives, Mrs. Eliza Van Lew's letter to her son, John.

19. "Occasional Journal," 2.

20. Ibid.

21. Ibid., 11.

22. Albee and William Gilmore Beymer, "Miss Van Lew," *Harper's Monthly Magazine,* vol. 123, June 1911.

23. *Richmond Enquirer,* July 31, 1861.

24. Alfred Ely, *The Journal of Alfred Ely,* 158–60.

25. Ibid., 163.

26. Pauline Revere Thayer, *A Memorial to Paul Joseph Revere and Edward H. R. Revere,* 82–83.

27. "Occasional Journal," n.p.

28. Robert W. Waitt, "Thomas McNiven Papers," n.p. His memoirs were told to his daughter Jeannette McNiven and recorded by Waitt, McNiven's grandson.

    Mary Elizabeth Bowser left Richmond after the war, and nothing further is known of her whereabouts. Mrs. McEva Bowser reported in a November 23, 1993, interview with the author that she believes a notebook she threw out in 1952 when cleaning out her mother-in-law's house was a diary kept by Mary Elizabeth Bowser. It was a small book of handwritten pages with the name "Davis" frequently written and had "1860s dates," she said. On June 30, 1995, Mary Elizabeth Bowser was inducted into the U.S. Army's Intelligence Hall of Fame during ceremonies at Fort Huachuca, Arizona.

29. "Occasional Journal," n.p.

30. Van Lew Papers, New York Public Library, General George G. Meade's February 4, 1864, letter to Mr. Babcock.

31. David D. Ryan, *Cornbread and Maggots, Cloak and Dagger: Union Prisoners and Spies in Civil War Richmond,* 143.

32. "Occasional Journal," n.p.

33. Ryan, 147.

34. Lieutenant R. Bartley, "The Kilpatrick-Dahlgren Raid against Richmond," *Southern Historical Society Papers,* vol. 13, 519.

35. Ibid., 520.

36. Clifford Dowdey and Louis H. Manarin, *The Wartime Papers of R. E. Lee,* Order No. 640, 678.

37. Van Lew Papers, New York Public Library, letter written after 1885 to an unidentified person.
38. "Occasional Journal," n.p.
39. The $1,500 in Confederate money was equal to $75 in U.S. money. Van Lew Papers, Virginia Historical Society, n.p., and "Confederate Inflation Chart," Official Publication No. 13, Richmond Civil War Centennial Commission.
40. Van Lew Papers, New York Public Library, n.p.
41. *Private and Official Correspondence of General Benjamin F. Butler during the Period of the Civil War,* vol. 3, 561.
42. Waitt, n.p.
43. Butler, 564.
44. Van Lew Papers, New York Public Library, n.p.
45. Ibid., Wickam's February 26, 1877, letter to Elizabeth.
46. Ibid., Grant's February 26, 1877, letter to Elizabeth.
47. Ibid., Elizabeth's April 10, 1877, letter to William K. Rogers.
48. Ibid., Elizabeth's March 26, 1881, letter in response to the *Washington Evening Star* comment.
49. Van Lew Papers, Swem Library, n.p.
50. Van Lew Papers, New York Public Library, Elizabeth's July 11, 1887, letter to "Gentlemen."
51. Ibid., n.p.
52. "Occasional Journal," New York Public Library, n.p.
53. John Albee, "Elizabeth Van Lew Papers," n.p.

1861

1. Salisbury, North Carolina, prison.
2. John Van Lew purchased his mansion at 24th and East Grace Streets in 1836 from Dr. John Adams.
3. Elizabeth is probably referring to her father's first unsuccessful business attempt. He was highly successful in his second attempt, operating a hardware business, and eventually he owned five stores.
4. Henry A. Wise was governor of Virginia from 1856 to 1860. He was appointed brigadier general on June 5, 1861, and raised a legion in western Virginia, serving there and at Roanoke

Island, North Carolina. Mark M. Boatner III, *The Civil War Dictionary,* 944.

5. James Johnston Pettigrew led Confederate troops in the take-over of Castle Pinckney and the fortification of Morris Island, after Union Major Robert Anderson occupied Fort Sumter. Pettigrew was promoted to brigadier general in 1862 and was wounded while leading his brigade during Pickett's Charge at Gettysburg, June 3, 1863. He was mortally wounded July 13 at what is now Falling Waters, West Virginia. Boatner, 649.

6. Edmund Ruffin, a Hanover County, Virginia, farmer and seces-sionist agitator, fired one of the first shots at Fort Sumter. Boat-ner, 712.

7. John Minor Botts was an unremitting foe of secession. Because of his activities, he was arrested and held for eight weeks in Castle Godwin, originally the McDaniel's Negro Jail, which was used to hold loyalists like Botts and military miscreants. Anderson, 30–37.

8. John Tyler was U.S. president from 1841 to 1845.

9. The flag took its name from Palmetto, South Carolina, where it was made. Boatner, 618.

10. The Farmers Market was located in Shockoe Bottom. Brown & Peasley was located on Seventeenth Street between Franklin and Grace Streets. A seafood store, it was operated by John and William Brown and William L. Peasley. 1866 *Richmond City Directory.*

11. "John Sescher" was an unkind name given by Elizabeth to Governor John Letcher, who was elected Virginia governor in 1860. A Unionist, he called for a national convention to dis-cuss ways of calming the mounting animosity between the North and the South. His suggestion was ignored. After six cotton states seceded in 1861 and Jefferson Davis was named Southern president, Letcher called a special session of the Vir-ginia General Assembly. That legislature invited the then thirty-four states remaining in the Union to a peace conference in Washington. "It was a complete failure," said Richmond

historian Virginius Dabney. Nevertheless, Letcher had tried to prevent Virginia's secession, contrary to Elizabeth's statement that he had "surrendered the State." Virginius Dabney, *Richmond: The Story of a City*, 160–62.

12. Fort Sumter was fired on by the Confederates at Charleston Harbor in South Carolina, on April 12, 1861. Union Major Robert Anderson officially surrendered the fort two days later. It is unclear to what Carlisle refers. E. B. Long and Barbara Long, *The Civil War Day by Day*, 56–57.

13. At least four members of the Sixth Massachusetts and nine civilians were killed at Baltimore on April 19, 1861, when prosecessionists attacked the Massachusetts troops as they were changing trains for Washington. Long, 62.

14. The Virginia Convention voted April 17, 1861, to secede from the Union. Long, 60.

15. John McGill was the Roman Catholic Bishop of Richmond from 1850 to 1872. Records of the Catholic Diocese of Richmond.

16. Mrs. Ricketts was the wife of Union General James B. Ricketts. He was wounded, captured at the First Battle of Bull Run, and held prisoner in Richmond for six months. His wife treated him at Harwood Prison, where she met Elizabeth. Boatner, 699, and "Occasional Journal," n.p.

17. Mayor Joseph Mayo.

18. The Battle of Bethel Church, Virginia, also known as the Battle of Big Bethel, took place on June 10, 1861, about eight miles west of Hampton. Colonel J. Bankhead Magruder commanded the Confederate forces at Bethel Church. *Battles and Leaders of the Civil War*, Vol. 1, 174, and *Richmond Whig*, June 13, 1861.

19. Private Henry L. Wyatt was a member of the First North Carolina Infantry. *Richmond Whig*, June 13, 1861.

20. Ligon's Warehouse and Tobacco Factory was used as the first prison. It was located at the corner of Twenty-fifth and Main Streets. Sandra V. Parker, *Richmond's Civil War Prisons*, 3–4.

21. Lieutenant David H. Todd, half brother of Mrs. Lincoln.

William H. Townsend, *Lincoln and the Bluegrass: Slavery and the Civil War in Kentucky,* 317–18.

22. Christopher Gustavus Memminger was Confederate Secretary of the Treasury. Boatner, 542.

23. The Custom House, built two years before the war by the Federal government, is the present-day post office and U.S. Court building at 1000 E. Main Street. Dabney, 192.

24. General John Henry Winder was Provost Marshal and in charge of the city's prisons. Boatner, 940–41.

25. Winder's original note said "Miss Van Lew," but the journal has a series of dots where her name should be. "Occasional Journal," n.p.

26. Charlotte Corday, a patriot during the French Revolution, was executed in 1793. *The New Encyclopedia Britannica,* vol. 3, 624.

27. Here Elizabeth is writing about the American flag being replaced by Confederate flags of different designs.

1862

1. Lieutenant Todd was relieved of duty and sent to an artillery unit. He died of wounds received at the battle of Vicksburg in 1863. Anderson, 30–37.

2. Aaron Burr was suspected of plotting to overthrow the U.S. government by creating a new government in western Virginia. He was arrested for treason and brought to Richmond for trial, but was acquitted. While in Richmond in 1807, he was held briefly at the Henrico Jail. Dabney, 71–73.

3. A. G. Bledsoe was assistant secretary of war.

4. Elizabeth was allowed to leave food and books for the prisoners at Libby, but she could not enter the building.

5. Ill treatment of prisoners was not confined to the South. Approximately 27,000 Confederate soldiers died from sickness, maltreatment, and poor living conditions in Northern prisons. An estimated 30,200 Union prisoners died in prisons. William B. Hesseltine, *Civil War Prisons,* 256.

6. Henry Wirz was in charge of Richmond's Belle Isle Prison, and

later the Andersonville, Georgia, Prison. More than 13,000 Union prisoners died at the latter while he was in command. He was hanged by Federal officials after the war ended because of his administration of Andersonville, although some historians now believe he was used as a scapegoat. Parker, 15, and William Marvel, *Andersonville: The Last Depot,* 232–49.

7. Richard "Dick" Turner was the policeman at Libby Prison. He was very hard on the inmates, treating them with contempt, and was mentioned with hatred in prisoners' diaries. Thomas P. Turner's letter to Mrs. Sale, Virginia Historical Society; Louis Palma Di Cesnola, *Ten Months in Libby Prison,* 2; and Parker, 11.

8. No record could be found of the Rev. Dr. Styles's first name.

9. Elizabeth may be referring to Captain Edward P. Alexander, who was Chief of Ordnance under General Beauregard at the Battle of Seven Pines.

10. Captain Archibald C. Godwin was provost marshal and in charge of Castle Godwin, a prison for civilians and Federal and Confederate deserters. He was also commander of Salisbury Prison in North Carolina. Arch Fredric Blakey, *General John H. Winder, C.S.A.,* 121.

11. A number of Carrington cousins lived on Church Hill and were friends and neighbors of the Van Lews. Apparently Elizabeth is referring to one of them, mentioning her several times in the journal, but never giving her first name.

12. John Minor Botts had a farm in Hanover County near Mechanicsville. "Occasional Journal," n.p., and 1865 Confederate Army Engineer's map of Richmond.

13. On Christmas morning 1861, Timothy Webster left Washington for his third trip to Richmond, and by the middle of January was back in the nation's capital with a large bundle of mail he had stolen. It contained letters and dispatches written by Secretary of War Judah P. Benjamin, General John H. Winder, and others high in the Confederate administration. Again he returned to Richmond, this time with Hattie Lewis, who worked for the U.S. Secret Service. They crossed the Potomac

in late January and were not heard from for weeks. Two of Pinkerton's other detectives, Pryce Lewis and John Scully, were sent to Richmond to hunt for them. They found them in a hotel. Webster was ill and emaciated, suffering from his long-term illness, rheumatism. Hattie had been nursing him. Webster tried to warn Lewis and Scully that they all were being watched, and the next day Lewis and Scully were arrested and thrown in the Henrico Jail. Lewis escaped during a breakout with fellow prisoners only to be recaptured. Both were imprisoned for twenty-two months. Hattie Lewis was imprisoned for a year. Elizabeth was incorrect in referring to Hattie as Webster's wife; although she was in love with him and nursed him, Hattie was not his wife. Webster, one of Pinkerton's favorite detectives and a friend of General George McClellan, was hanged on April 29, 1862. William Gilmore Beymer, *On Hazardous Service,* 259–87.

14. Mr. William P. Wood was the keeper of the Old Capital Prison in Washington, D.C., and was in Richmond exchanging prisoners. *Official Records,* Series 2, vol. 4, 654.

15. George Welch was one of several Federal soldiers taken prisoner in western Virginia and held at Castle Thunder.

16. Spencer Kellogg was a fourth master on Union Admiral W. D. Porter's ship, *USS Essex.* He and four other *Essex* seamen were captured by Confederate guerrillas on August 15, 1862, while cutting adrift flatboats used by the Confederates to take supplies across the Mississippi River at New Orleans. The other Webster was Charles W. Webster, a civilian, accused of spying for the Union. *O.R.,* Series 2, vol. 4, 503, and Series 2, vol. 6, 339.

1863

1. No record could be found of Bishop Polk's first name nor the religious denomination he represented.

2. Commander Charles O. Boutelle, U.S. Coast Survey Office, Washington, D.C. *Official Records,* Series 1, vol. 6, 4, and Series 1, vol. 47, Part 3, 572.

3. Butler refers here to the hidden message on such letters, which became visible after heat was applied. He sent one of his spies, William S. Rowley, who lived on a Henrico County farm, to Elizabeth to show her how to use invisible ink, lemon juice, on her letters to Butler, and how to apply heat to Butler's letters. Butler, 319.

1864

1. Perhaps William S. Rowley, who was one of the first spies working for Thomas McNiven. McNiven Papers, n.p.
2. Rockett's Landing.
3. Robert W. Waitt reports his aunt, Jeannette McNiven, told him that her father, Thomas McNiven, said he was "Quaker." Waitt made a record of the stories his grandfather told Jeannette McNiven about his spy activities in Richmond during the war. Thomas McNiven worked out of a bakery on North Eighth Street and said his customers included the Jefferson Davis family. McNiven was a small man, barely five feet tall, with beady eyes and a walrus mustache. A photograph taken after the war shows him and other loyalists seated below the A. P. Hill monument in Richmond, celebrating the Union victory, as they did annually. McNiven claimed to have recruited several hundred Union spies from among the loyalists in Richmond. Only the name "Quaker" is found in the *Official Records,* but like Elizabeth, McNiven said he requested the U.S. War Department to return to him all records of his activities during the war. He destroyed them. Waitt, Thomas McNiven Papers.
4. This "Mr. Palmer" may have been the Charles S. Palmer identified by Union spy Thomas McNiven as a loyalist who helped McNiven. Palmer owned a farm adjacent to William S. Rowley's farm off the Mechanicsville Turnpike, a few miles northeast of Richmond. Rowley worked as a spy for General Butler. McNiven Papers, n.p.; 1865 Confederate Army Engineer's map of Richmond; and Butler's Letters, 520.
5. Chaffin's Bluff and Drewry's Bluff were located on the banks

of the James River between Richmond and Petersburg. *Battles and Leaders,* vol. 4, 206–12.

6. White House Landing was located on the Pamunkey River east of Richmond. *Battles and Leaders,* vol. 4, 206–12.

7. Mr. Holmes is not identified by Elizabeth, but he was probably one of her loyalist friends. The name Mr. Holmes may have been a code name to hide the spy's identity. Code names were used by Elizabeth and General Butler in their correspondence with each other. "Occasional Journal," n.p., and Butler, 521.

8. Chaffin's Farm was located off State Route 5 (the Varina Road) in eastern Henrico County near Fort Harrison. It was the site of a battle on September 29, 1864, in which troops under Union Generals David B. Birney and E. O. C. Ord took Chaffin's Farm and Fort Harrison. The 20,000 Union soldiers included the Third Negro Division, whose members fought gallantly. Union casualties numbered more than 3,000. The 11,000 Confederate defenders had an estimated 2,000 casualties. G. J. Fiebger, *Campaigns of the American Civil War,* 303, and Boatner, 588–89.

9. Elizabeth is apparently referring to Mrs. Graves as being a Confederate woman spy. She is not identified by Elizabeth nor is she mentioned in the *Official Records.*

10. General Butler did not attack Richmond.

11. McNiven Papers, n.p.; "Occasional Journal," n.p.; *Harper's Monthly Magazine,* vol. 123, June 1911, No. 733; and Ryan, 143.

12. Roberts was apparently an out-of-city attorney. He was not listed in the *Richmond City Directories* for the war period or after and is not identified further in any of Elizabeth's papers.

13. *New York Times,* February 17, 1864.

14. Howard's Grove was a neighborhood located on the Mechansville Turnpike east of the city. 1865 Confederate Army Engineer's map of Richmond and McNiven Papers, n.p.

15. Mrs. Greer was Mrs. Abbie Greer, according to an account in the *History of the 51st Indiana,* published in 1894, 170–74.

16. The account in the *History of the 51st Indiana* identified her as Mrs. L. A. Rice. *History of the 51st Indiana,* 170–74.

17. Major Bedan B. McDonald, 101st Ohio, was one of the tunnel work party, and spent many hours digging it. Miss Van Lew did not identify the other two escapees. However, an account in the *History of the 51st Indiana* identifies them as Captain William Scearce and Lieutenant John Sterling, Thirtieth Indiana. After getting out of the tunnel, Colonel Streight and Captain Scearce, joined by Major McDonald and Lieutenant Sterling, went to the home of a black woman as Mrs. Greer had directed. Mrs. Greer then took them to her house at Howard's Grove, where they stayed for a week before successfully making their way to Union lines. *History of the 51st Indiana,* 170–74, and "Occasional Journal," n.p.

18. One hundred and three prisoners escaped and fifty-two were recaptured. Ryan, 145.

19. Major Bedan B. McDonald was promoted to lieutenant colonel on February 26, 1864, and mustered out at the end of the war. *The Official Roster of the Soldiers of the State of Ohio in the War of the Rebellion,* 1861–66, vol. 7, 477.

20. "Know, O peoples, and be appalled! Give ear, all you distant lands! Arm, but be crushed! Arm, but be crushed! Form a plan, and it shall be thwarted; make a resolve, and it shall not be carried out, for 'With us is God!' For thus said the Lord to me, taking hold of me and warning me not to walk in the way of this people: Call not alliance what this people calls alliance, and fear not, nor stand in awe of what they fear. But with the Lord of hosts make your alliance—for him be your fear and your awe." Isaiah 8: 9–13.

21. The February 20, 1864, edition of the *Richmond Examiner* could not be found in the Virginia State Library and Archives, the Alderman Library at the University of Virginia, or the Library of Congress. However, the February 20, 1864, edition of the *Richmond Enquirer* carries an account, "Execution of a Yankee Spy," that verifies the facts Elizabeth quotes from the *Examiner.*

22. Adjutant Wiley. No further information could be found in any existing record.

23. Elizabeth refers to the black guide, Martin Robinson, who led Colonel Dahlgren to a point on the James River west of Richmond, where the guide had told Dahlgren he could cross. The river, however, was too high. Dahlgren had planned to cross and head up the south bank and take Belle Isle, free the prisoners there, and then cross the Mayo Bridge into the city. Angry that his plan was foiled, he ordered Robinson hanged.

24. Dahlgren was ambushed on March 1 by members of Company H, Ninth Virginia, under Lieutenant James Pollard, a part of Fitzhugh Lee's division, and members of Company E, Fifth Virginia, under Captain E. C. Fox. *Southern Historical Society Papers,* vol. 13, 531, and Alfred Bagby, King and Queen County, Virginia, 70–75.

25. None of the *Official Records* list Magruder's first name. He was likely John William Magruder, who spent four months at Virginia Military Institute and fought with "Stonewall" Jackson. He was a courier for R. E. Lee's Headquarters during the winter of 1863–64. He then joined the 7th Virginia Cavalry. (Research courtesy of John M. Coski, historian for the Museum of the Confederacy.) The "Col. McGruder" Elizabeth refers to was John Bankhead Magruder. Richard L. Armstrong, *7th Virginia Cavalry,* 189, and Boatner, 501.

26. The exact number of captured prisoners varies in reports from 92 to 135. Lieutenant Pollard gave the latter estimate: "Forty blacks and one hundred thirty-five soldiers." "Occasional Journal," n.p., and *Southern Historical Society Papers,* vol. 13, 530–31.

27. Elizabeth is referring to the Stevensville junction roads (State Routes 629 and 631), now known as Dahlgren's Corner. The Mantipike Ferry crossed the Mattaponi (Mattapony, as it was called then) River near the road junctions. *Southern Historical Society Papers,* vol. 13, 535, and *Virginia: A Guide to the Old Dominion,* 371.

28. Deceased Union soldiers were buried outside Oakwood Cemetery so as not to desecrate the hallowed ground where Confederate soldiers were buried.

29. F. W. E. Lohmann was one of Elizabeth's loyalist friends. "Occasional Journal," n.p., and *Southern Historical Society Papers,* vol. 13, 530–31.

30. Martin M. Lipscomb was also a member of the loyalist group that helped Miss Van Lew.

31. Elizabeth is writing about her own examination of the body.

32. It was actually Kilpatrick who fought there.

33. The Brook Turnpike. It ran north and south between Richmond and Washington, D.C.

34. The Lohmann brothers were F. W. E. and Eberhardt. McNiven Papers, n.p.

35. Yellow Tavern was a stage tavern located about five miles north of Richmond on the Brook Turnpike. General J. E. B. Stuart was mortally wounded near there on May 11, 1864, while defending against Union General Philip Sheridan's attempt to reach Richmond with 12,000 troopers. Stuart had only a quarter of the troops Sheridan had. Trying to rally his men, he rode into the midst of the afternoon fighting and was shot in the stomach by a dismounted cavalryman. He died the next day. "Stuart's death was a crippling blow to the future campaigning of the army," noted historian Clifford Dowdey in *R. E. Lee.* "Like ["Stonewall"] Jackson, the chief of cavalry was literally irreplaceable. . . ." Boatner, 951, and Clifford Dowdey, *Lee,* 456.

36. "Quick" was the code name for Robert Orrick, to whose farm in Glen Allen, Henrico County, Colonel Dahlgren's body was taken by Rowley. McNiven Papers, n.p.

37. According to accounts in the local newspapers and of Richmond diarist Sallie Ann Putnam, the papers found on Dahlgren's body reportedly said, "We hope to release the prisoners from Belle Island; . . . cross the James River into Richmond; destroy and burn the hateful city, and to not allow the rebel leader, Davis, and his traitorous crew to escape." Apparently the papers did exist, for General R. E. Lee was asked his opinion on their publication. He responded, "I concur with you in thinking that a formal publication of these papers should be

made under official authority, that our people & the world may know the character of the war our enemies wage against us, & the unchristian & atrocious acts they plot & perpetrate." *The Wartime Papers of R. E. Lee,* Order No. 640. When a small group of Union cavalrymen sent to guard Elizabeth April 3, 1865, found her, she was searching among the ruins of the War Department building, probably looking for the Dahlgren papers.

38. Elizabeth often bribed clerks in the Confederate War and Naval Departments for information, according to McNiven, Union Colonel D. B. Parker, and statements in her journal. "Occasional Journal," n.p., and McNiven Papers, n.p. Also see *New York Herald,* July 1, 1883.

39. Union General John Pope was hated by Southerners after directing his men to live off the countryside and placing strict controls over civilians who fell within Federal lines. In addition, noncombatants were held accountable for destruction of public or private property as well as for the infliction of bodily harm on Union troops. Boatner, 659, and Dowdey, 279.

40. Powder kegs were placed around Libby Prison after the prison escape February 9, 1864. The remaining prisoners were warned the kegs would be exploded if there were any more escape attempts. John Beauchamp Jones, *A Rebel War Clerk's Diary,* vol. II, 164.

41. This quote was taken by the *Whig* from the papers found on Dahlgren's body. His father, Admiral John Adolph Dahlgren, charged in his 1872 memoir of his son that the papers were forged, noting the signature was "U. Dalhgren." "The document alleged to have been found upon the person on Colonel Dahlgren is utterly discredited by the fact that the signature attached to it cannot possibly be his own because it is not his name—a letter is misplaced and the real name Dahlgren is spelled Dalhgren. . . . Colonel Dahlgren invariably signed himself 'Ulric Dahlgren,' never with the bare initial of the first name." From Admiral Dahlgren's book, *Memoir of Ulric Dahlgren,* quoted in *Southern Historical Society Papers,* vol. 13,

545. However, Virgil Carrington Jones, who made the most intensive study of the papers, was convinced they were genuine. Jones, *Eight Hours before Richmond,* 100, and note 37.

42. General Arnold Jones Elzey commanded the Department of Richmond from December 1862 until autumn 1864. Boatner, 264–65.

43. Dahlgren ordered his men to plunder and burn farms and mills as they moved through Goochland County toward the James River.

44. Dover was in Goochland County, and Atlee's Station was on the Meadowbridge Road in Hanover County. 1865 Confederate Army Engineer's map of Richmond.

45. Martin Meredith Libscomb was an undertaker and loyalist. McNiven Papers, n.p.

46. This part of the narrative is confusing. Apparently Elizabeth is saying Dahlgren's hat was taken from his body and kept by the stepson of the tavern owner at King & Queen Courthouse. The names of the tavern owner, his stepson, and the tavern could not be found in the King & Queen County records or histories. The tavern, courthouse, clerk's office, and private buildings were burned down during a raid May 10, 1864, by General Kilpatrick in retaliation for Dahlgren's death. The raid cost Kilpatrick more than 300 casualties. Rev. Alfred Bagby, *King and Queen County, Virginia,* 75.

47. Elizabeth is referring to General Fitz Lee's cavalrymen under Lieutenant James Pollard, Company H, Ninth Virginia Cavalry (General John Randolph Chambliss's brigade). *Southern Historical Society Papers,* vol. 13, 530–31.

48. B. Wardwell was a Richmond ice dealer who aided Elizabeth. McNiven Papers, n.p.

49. The Confederate Naval Yard at Richmond, which was located on the south bank of the James River across from Rockett's Landing, could be seen from Elizabeth's house. Ironclads and rams were serviced there, and Butler was asking Elizabeth to keep a watch on their movements.

50. Confederate General Edward "Allegheny" Johnson fought at the battles of the Wilderness and Spotsylvania, but was not killed. He was captured at Spotsylvania and exchanged a short time later. General Zebulon Baird Vance, former governor of North Carolina, also was not killed during the battle of Spotsylvania. Boatner, 437–38.

51. Higgins was apparently one of Miss Van Lew's loyalist friends, but she does not identify him further.

52. Drewry's Bluff is located south of Richmond on the south bank of the James River. It was being threatened by Butler's troops even as Grant was fighting Lee north of Richmond. Boatner, 247–49.

53. Drewry's Bluff and Chaffin's Bluff were under attack by Butler's troops. Butler drove the Confederates from Drewry's Bluff May 12, but Chaffin's Bluff still remained in the hands of the rebels. Boatner, 247–49.

54. The woods at the Wilderness caught fire from the rifle flashes, and hundreds of wounded Union soldiers burned to death. *Battles and Leaders,* vol. 4, 162.

55. Nelson was one of Elizabeth's servants. He was believed to have been the father of Mary Elizabeth Bowser, the servant who worked in the Davis Mansion. Author's interview with Mrs. McEva Bowser, Mary Elizabeth Bowser's great-niece.

56. This entry was written one week after the battle of Spotsylvania. Lee had moved his troops south to the North Anna to block Grant, and the fighting continued there. The next major battle would take place at Cold Harbor in eastern Hanover County in four days, June 1 through 3. At 4:30 A.M. June 3, the Federals launched an attack on the Confederates' zigzag defenses in one of the bloodiest fights of the war. An estimated 7,000 Federal soldiers were cut down by fire from three directions in eight to ten minutes. Some Federal officers refused to send their men into another charge when it was ordered later that day. Captain Thomas E. Barker, commander of the Twelfth New Hampshire, wrote after the battle that he

responded to the order with a shout: "I will not take my regiment in another such charge if Jesus Christ himself should order it!" *Battles and Leaders*, vol. 4, 213–32, and Geoffrey C. Ward, *The Civil War*, 294.

57. Detective New's message was one of the ones Elizabeth retrieved from the U.S. War Department in 1866. She kept this one but destroyed the others, which were her responses for information from Generals Butler, Sharpe, and Grant.

58. Mrs. Eliza Van Lew, Elizabeth's mother.

59. Libby Prison. John Albee, a Boston researcher, recorded a conversation he had with two unidentified former Libby prisoners: "Nearly every Sunday morning they used to see her walk down the hill towards the prison and then turn along the street in front and pass by. She sometimes carried an empty pitcher and then again would carelessly raise her handkerchief to her face, meanwhile, however, never looking towards the prison. The negroes who came in to scrub, would say, 'That is Miss Van Lew. She will be a friend if you can escape.' . . . The constant suspicion by the authorities necessitated equally constant vigilance by Miss Van Lew." John Albee Papers, Swem Library, College of William and Mary.

1865

1. Lemuel E. Babcock was a native of Massachusetts. He moved to Virginia in 1850, briefly living in Surry County, and, in the late 1850s, moved to eastern Charles City County. There he acquired land and slaves and established himself as a successful lumber merchant. Despite his Unionist sympathies, Babcock remained in Virginia after the outbreak of the war and tried to live harmoniously with his neighbors. Nevertheless, local authorities charged him in 1862 "with reading abolishionary [*sic*]" papers to slaves, but dismissed the charges for lack of evidence. After a second arrest in Richmond in 1864 on charges of being a "suspicious character," Babcock became a spy and guide for the Federal army. The scheme to plant another spy in

the Confederate capital led to his arrest and imprisonment. Shortly before the Confederate evacuation of the city, Babcock was put on a train for Danville, but he escaped in Amelia County. He returned to Charles City after the war and was elected by the black majority to the state constitutional convention. He deeded his sawmill to his son in 1871 and moved with his wife in 1872 to Albans, Vermont. Research courtesy of John M. Coski.

2. McNiven Papers, n.p.

3. This spy may have been Thomas McNiven. He was in the employ of Union General George H. Sharpe, an aide to General Ulysses S. Grant. Sharpe ran the Union spy effort. With his Scottish citizenship papers and papers identifying him as a buyer for the P. Lorillard Tobacco Company, McNiven moved easily and often through the Confederate lines. McNiven Papers, n.p.

4. Jordan Rugfel was apparently a loyalist friend. No further information is found in Elizabeth's papers or the *Official Records*.

5. The word "Oyates" probably refers to oysters. Robert Dudley, who sold oysters from a store opposite the Farmers' Market, was a loyalist friend. No saloon by that name existed in Richmond during the war, according to city records.

6. The Spotswood Hotel was located at Eighth and Main Streets. Dabney, 218.

7. Detective Reese's first name could not be found in any official record.

8. Samuel B. Maccubbin was General Winder's chief detective. Blakey, *General John H. Winder, C.S.A.,* 122.

9. Both the *Richmond Enquirer* and the *Richmond Daily Dispatch* of February 27, 1865, and the *Official Records* (Series 2, vol. 8, 207) identify the Federal spy as R. W. Pool. The *Official Records* identified him as a first lieutenant with the 113th Illinois before coming to Richmond. In addition to Babcock, William White, described by the *Enquirer* as being "a detailed conscript living in

the Eastern portion of the city and who was represented as a good Union man," was betrayed by Pool and put in Castle Thunder as a spy.

10. James M. Mason and John Slidell were Confederate diplomats. Boatner, 847. They were on their way to England aboard the British mail steamer *Trent,* when the ship was intercepted by the *USS San Jacinto* on November 8, 1861. They were arrested and taken to Boston. The Confederate government protested the arrests and held two Federal prisoners hostage for the diplomats. Both the diplomats and prisoners were later freed.

11. Babcock had escaped before the Union soldiers arrived. See note 1.

12. The Union army took Richmond the morning of April 3, 1865. "We took Richmond at a quarter past eight this morning," General Godfrey Weitzel telegraphed General Grant. Godfrey Weitzel, *Richmond Occupied,* 54.

13. The Gallego and Haxal Flour Mills.

CONCLUSION

1. Butler's letters, 564.

2. Van Lew Papers, New York Public Library, General George H. Sharpe's January 1867 letter to General Cyrus Ballou Comstock.

3. Franklin Stearns was a liquor dealer. He was jailed briefly because of his loyalist statements. A month after Richmond surrendered, Stearns was named as a director of the new First National Bank of Richmond, which was financed primarily by Northern stockholders. 1860 *Richmond City Directory* and Dabney, 201, 210.

4. Sergeant Erasmus Ross, a clerk at Libby Prison, was mentioned frequently in the diaries of Union prisoners as a vile and mean man, wearing two pistols and damning all Yankees. He worked for the Danville Depot after the war and died in

the 1870 Spotswood Hotel fire. *Richmond Dispatch,* July 17, 1883.

5. *Richmond Evening Journal,* May 2, 1908.

APPENDIX: SELECTED LETTERS

1. General Butler is referring to money to finance the espionage activities in Richmond, some of which Holmes carried through the lines for him. Butler's March 22, 1864, letter to William Rowley.

2. Elizabeth is believed to have used the cipher long before the summer of 1864, as Sharpe claimed. William Gilmore Beymer, "Miss Van Lew," *Harper's Monthly Magazine,* vol. 123, June 1911, 88.

3. Colonel S. M. Bowman, Fifteenth Massachusetts; Colonel Milton Cogswell (spelled Coggswell in some records), Forty-second New York; Captain Hugh W. McQuade, Thirty-eighth New York; and Congressman Alfred Ely were prisoners in Richmond's Harwood Prison in 1861. Cogswell was also held as a hostage in the Henrico Jail with Major Paul Joseph Revere. Captain Edward H. Chase, Co. D, 110th U.S. Colored Troops, was held at Libby Prison in 1864. Paul Revere Thayer, *A Memorial of Paul Joseph Revere and Edward H. R. Revere,* 100–105, and Alfred Ely, *The Diary of Alfred Ely,* 215–16.

4. Citizen E. B. Boutwell was a prisoner in Richmond in early 1862. Upon release, he feared arrest again and went to Elizabeth, who hid him in her home. No further information is known about Boutwell. *O.R.,* Series 2, vol. 2, 340.

5. Lieutenant Colonel I. Harris Hooper, Fifteenth Massachusetts, was captured at Gettysburg. He was held prisoner in Richmond's Libby Prison for several months. *Massachusetts Soldiers, Sailors and Marines in the Civil War,* vol. 3, 199.

6. General Marsena Rudolph Patrick was Union provost marshal in Richmond from May 25 to June 9, 1865.

7. Colonel Theodore S. Bowers served as an assistant adjutant general on Grant's staff. *Battles and Leaders,* vol. 4, 740.

8. Charles S. Palmer, Robert Dudley, and Horace Kent were Richmond loyalists. McNiven Papers, n.p.

9. Dr. George K. Gilmer served in the Virginia House of Delegates from 1869 to 1871. W. Asbury Christin, *Richmond—Her Past and Present*, 305–6, and *Richmond Dispatch*, July 2, 1877.

10. John Grubbs worked in the Richmond Post Office with Elizabeth. He was also a neighbor of Thomas McNiven. Elizabeth is referring to the situtation in which no Richmond bank was willing to loan her money on her house because of her political views and espionage during the war. McNiven Papers, n.p., and "Occasional Journal," n.p.

11. Lieutenant James Ruth was a member of the 121st Pennsylvania, Company I. He was wounded and captured at Gettysburg July 2, 1863, and held prisoner in Richmond's Libby Prison. *O. R.,* Series 1, vol. 27, 323–24, and Bates, Samuel R. *History of Pennsylvania Volunteers,* vol. 4, 50.

12. Elizabeth and her niece, Elizabeth Louise Klapp, the daughter of Elizabeth's sister, Anna Paulina Van Lew Klapp. Miss Klapp cared for her aunt in the last years of Miss Van Lew's life. Omohundra, 654.

13. Dr. Hunter Holmes McGuire, a noted Richmond doctor, was personal physician to General "Stonewall" Jackson. Dowdey, 352.

BIBLIOGRAPHY

MANUSCRIPTS
College of William and Mary, Williamsburg, Virginia
    Elizabeth Van Lew Papers
    John Albee Papers
Czechoslovak Heritage Museum Library and Archives, Berwyn,
    Illinois
    Thomas Pratt Turner Letter
Dan Duke, Eaton, Ohio
    Edward Cottingham Letter
Bettie Terrell Dorsey, Richmond, Virginia
    Elizabeth Van Lew "Workbook"
National Archives, Washington, D.C.
    Record Group 217
    Lemuel E. Babcock Petition to Southern Claims Commission
    John Donally, Incident Report
    A. S. Dallas Letter to J. R. Leslie concerning the escape of
        Private Charles E. Pine
New York Public Library, Rare Books and Manuscripts Division,
    Astor, Lenox, and Tilden Foundations
    Elizabeth Van Lew Papers
Scott C. Newkirk, Mickleton, N.J.
    John C. Digman Military Record
Ohio Historical Society, Columbus
    Joseph N. Potts Letters
    Nelson Purdum Papers
    Andrew Roy Papers

James W. Vance Andersonville Diary
William T. Wilson Papers
University of North Carolina, Chapel Hill
Charles Carroll Gray Diary
Virginia Historical Society, Richmond
Elizabeth Van Lew Papers
Thomas Pratt Turner Letter
Samuel A. Urquhart Letter
Virginia State Library and Archives, Richmond
George W. Libby Letter
John Van Lew Letter
Eliza Van Lew Letter
Robert W. Waitt, Richmond, Virginia
Thomas McNiven Papers
"The Libby Prison Minstrels!" December 24, 1863

NEWPAPERS
"A Soldier's Protest." *New York Times,* February 23, 1888.
"Again in Libby Prison." *New York Times,* March 29, 1891.
"Arrival of Escaped Union Officers at Yorktown." *New York Times,* February 16, 1864.
"The Big Break-out from Libby." *Baltimore Sun Magazine,* July 1960.
"Calls It a Vile Scheme." *New York Times,* February 11, 1888.
"Capture of Col. Rose." *Camden (S. C.) Chronicle,* June 26, 1914.
"Change of Administration." *Richmond Dispatch,* July 2, 1877.
"Concerning the Raid on Richmond." *New York Times,* March 11, 1864.
"The Condition of Our Prisoners in Richmond." *New York Times,* March 4, 1864.
"Days and Nights of Doubt." *New York Times,* March 22, 1891.
"The Escaped Prisoners." *Washington Star,* February 16, 1864.
"The First Night in Libby." *New York Times,* February 15, 1891.
"Getting Away from Libby." *New York Times,* February 22, 1891.

"The Hostages for the Privateersmen." *Richmond Whig,* November 14, 1861.

"Hungry Days and Nights." *New York Times,* March 8, 1891.

"In Southern War Prisons." *New York Times,* February 8, 1891.

"The Libby Deed Recorded." *Richmond Dispatch,* February 28, 1888.

"Libby Prison." *Richmond Dispatch,* February 7, 1888.

"The Libby Prison. Confession That the Prison Was Mined." *Richmond Dispatch,* March 24, 1864.

"Libby Prison Again Sold." *New York Times,* September 21, 1888.

"Libby Prison in Ruins." *New York Times,* May 8, 1889.

"The Libby Prison Removal." *Richmond Dispatch,* February 10, 1888.

"Libby Prison Sale." *Richmond Dispatch,* February 11, 1888.

"Libby Prison Sale." *Richmond Dispatch,* February 15, 1888.

"Libby Prison Sale." *Richmond Dispatch,* February 24, 1888.

"Libby Prison Sold." *New York Times,* February 26, 1888.

"The Libby Prison Syndicate." *New York Times,* October 26, 1888.

"Libby Prison to Be Torn Down." *New York Times,* February 26, 1888.

"Libby Prison to Court." *New York Times,* June 3, 1897.

"Libby Prison's Tunnel." *New York Times,* March 8, 1888.

"The Libby's Removal." *Richmond Dispatch,* May 11, 1889.

"Life in Libby Prison." *New York Times,* February 1, 1891.

"Local Matters." *Richmond Dispatch,* April 13, 1877.

"Major Turner's Escape." *New York Times,* July 7, 1895.

"Mary Elizabeth Bowser." *Bronx (N.Y.) Press-Review,* October 20, 1977.

"Prisoners on Belle Isle." *New York Times,* March 1, 1891.

"Reported Escape of One Hundred and Nine Union Officers." *New York Times,* February 15, 1864.

"The Richmond Spy. How Miss Van Lew and Other Richmond Citizens Aided General Grant." *Richmond Dispatch,* July 17, 1883.

"To Exhibit Libby Prison." *New York Times,* February 23, 1888.
"Tunnelling to Freedom." *New York Times,* March 22, 1891.

BOOKS

Annual Report of the Adjutant General of the State of New York for the Year of 1899, Serial 1–146. Albany, N.Y., 1899.

Armstrong, Richard L. *The Virginia Cavalry.* Lynchburg, Va., 1992.

Bagby, Alfred. *King and Queen County, Virginia.* New York, 1908.

Bates, Samuel P. *History of Pennsylvania Volunteers.* Vols 1–6. Harrisburg, Pa., 1869.

Battles and Leaders of the Civil War. 4 Vols. New York, 1887–88.

Beatty, John. *The Citizen-Soldier: Memories of a Volunteer.* Cincinnati, 1879.

Beers, Frederic W. *Illustrated Atlas of the City of Richmond, Va.* Richmond, 1876.

Bill, Alfred Hoyt. *The Beleaguered City, Richmond 1861–1865.* New York, 1946.

Blackett, R. J. M., ed. *Thomas Morris Chester, Black Civil War Correspondent: His Dispatches from the Virginia Front.* Baton Rouge, La., 1989.

Blakey, Arch Fredric. *General John H. Winder C.S.A.* Gainesville, Fla., 1990.

Booth, B. F. *Dark Days of the Rebellion. Life in Southern Military Prisons.* Indianola, Iowa, 1897.

Botts, John Minor. *The Great Rebellion: Its Secret History, Rise, Progress, and Disastrous Failure.* New York, 1866.

Boykin, E. M. *The Falling Flag—Evacuation of Richmond, Retreat and Surrender at Appomattox.* New York, 1874.

Burns, A. Bohmer, ed. *Register of Interments, January 1, 1851–December 31, 1950, Shockoe Hill Cemetery, Richmond, Va.* Richmond, 1960.

Cavado, F. F. *Libby Life: Experiences of a Prisoner of War in Richmond, Va.* Philadelphia, 1865.

Chesnut, Mary Boykin Miller. *A Diary from Dixie.* New York, 1905.

Chesterman, William D. *Guide to Richmond and the Battle-Fields.* Richmond, 1894.

Christian, W. Ashbury. *Richmond—Her Past and Present.* Richmond, 1912.

Corcoran, Michael. *The Captivity of General Corcoran.* Philadelphia, 1864.

Coulter, E. Merton. *The Confederate States of America, 1861–1865.* 7 Vols. Baton Rouge, La., 1950.

Dabney, Virginius. *Richmond: The Story of a City.* Garden City, N.Y., 1976.

Dahlgren, John A. *Virginia, the New Dominion.* Garden City, N.Y. 1971.
———. *Memoir of Ulric Dahlgren.* Philadelphia, 1872.

Davis, Burke. *To Appomattox: Nine Days in April 1865.* New York, 1959.

Davis, Varina Howell. *Jefferson Davis, Ex-President of the Confederate States of America: A Memoir of His Wife.* 2 Vols. New York, 1890.

Dawson, Henry B. *The First Flag over Richmond, Virginia, April 3, 1865.* Morrisianna, N.Y., Privately printed, 1865.

DeLeon, Thomas Cooper. *Four Years in Rebel Capitals.* Mobile, Ala., 1890.

Dew, Charles B. *Ironmaker of the Confederacy. Joseph B. Anderson and the Tredegar Iron Works.* New Haven, Conn., 1966.

Di Cesnola, Louis Palma. *Ten Months in Libby Prison.* Privately printed, 1865.

Dow, Neal. *The Reminiscences of Neal Dow.* Portland, Maine, 1898.

Dowdey, Clifford. *R. E. Lee.* New York, 1961.
———. *Experiment in Rebellion.* Garden City, N.Y., 1946.

Dowdey, Clifford, and Louis H. Manarin. *The Wartime Papers of R. E. Lee.* New York, 1961.

Duke, Maurice, and Daniel P. Jordan. *A Richmond Reader 1732–1983.* Chapel Hill, N.C., 1983.

Ellis, Edward S. *Library of American History.* Vols. 4 & 5. Cincinnati, 1895.

Estvan, Bela. *War Pictures of the South.* New York, 1863.

Fosdick, Charles. *Five Hundred Days in Rebel Prisons*. Bethany, Mo., 1887.

Francis, Charles L. *Narrative of a Private Soldier in the Volunteer Army of the United States, during a Portion of the Period Covered by the Great War of the Rebellion of 1861*. Brooklyn, 1879.

Freeman, Douglas S. *R. E. Lee, a Biography*. 4 Vols. New York, 1934–35.

Glazier, Willard W. *The Capture, the Prison Pen and the Escape. . . .* Albany, 1866.

Godfrey, Dr. C. E. *Sketch of Major Henry Washington Sawyer*. Trenton, 1907.

Goss, Warren Lee. *A Soldier's Story of His Captivity at Andersonville, Belle Isle, and Other Rebel Prisons*. Boston, 1871.

Gracey, Rev. S. S. *Annals of the Sixth Pennsylvania Cavalry*. Butler, Pa., 1868.

Hamilton, A. G. *Story of the Famous Tunnel Escape from Libby Prison*. New York, privately printed, 1895.

Harris, William C. *Prison-Life in the Tobacco Warehouses at Richmond*. Philadelphia, 1862.

Harrison, Constance Cary. *Recollections Grave and Gay*. New York, 1911.

Hine, Darlene Clark. *Black Women in America: An Historical Encyclopedia*. New York, 1993.

History and Roster of Maryland Volunteers, War of 1861–1865. Vol 1. Baltimore, 1898.

Jeffery, William H. *Richmond Prisons, 1861–1865*. Johnsbury, Vt., 1893.

Johnston, Captain I. W. *Four Months in Libby, and the Campaign against Atlanta*. Cincinnati, 1864.

Jones, John Beauchamp. *A Rebel War Clerk's Diary at the Confederate States Capital*. 2 Vols. New York, 1935.

Jones, Katherine M. *Ladies of Richmond, Confederate Capital*. New York, 1962.

Journal of the Congress of the Confederate States of America. Washington, D.C., 1904.

Kane, Harnett T. *Spies of the Blue and Gray.* New York, 1954.

Kimmel, Stanley P. *Mr. Davis' Richmond.* New York, 1958.

Lewis, Samuel E., M.D. *The Treatment of Prisoners-of-War, 1861–1865.* Richmond, 1910.

Linn, Minnie V. *Dr. Hugh H. Linn.* Mangalore, S. India, 1950.

Lossing, Benson J. *Pictorial History of the Civil War in the United States.* 3 Vols. Philadelphia, 1866–69.

McCarty, C. *Walks about Richmond.* Richmond, 1870.

Manarin, Louis H., ed. *Richmond at War: The Minutes of the City Council, 1861–1865.* Chapel Hill, N.C., 1961.

Marks, Rev. J. J., D.D. *The Peninsula Campaign in Virginia.* Philadelphia, 1864.

Marvel, William. *Andersonville: The Last Depot.* Chapel Hill, N.C., 1994.

Massachusetts Soldiers, Sailors and Marines in the Civil War. 8 Vols. Boston, 1937.

Michigan Soldiers and Sailors Individual Records. Lansing, Mich., 1915.

Miller, Francis Trevelyan. *Photographic History of the Civil War.* Vol. 7. New York, 1911.

Moran, Captain Frank L. *A Thrilling History of the Famous Underground Tunnel of Libby Prison.* New York, 1889–93.

Official Roster of the Soldiers of the State of Ohio in the War of Rebellion, 1861–1866. Vols. 1–12, Akron, Ohio, 1893.

Omohundro, Malvern Hill. *The Omohundro Genealogical Record. The Omohundros and Allied Families in America.* Staunton, Va., privately printed, 1950–51.

Otis, George H. *Second Wisconsin Infantry.* Dayton, 1984.

Parker, Sandra V. *Richmond's Civil War Prisons.* Lynchburg, Va., 1990.

Patrick, Rembert W. *The Fall of Richmond.* Baton Rouge, La., 1960.

Pierson, Charles Lawrence. *Ball's Bluff: An Episode and Its Consequences to Us.* Salem, Mass., 1913.

Private and Official Correspondence of General Benjamin F. Butler during the Period of the Civil War. Vol. 3. Norwood, Mass., 1917.

Putnam, George Haven. *A Prisoner of War in Virginia, 1864–65.* New York, 1912.

Putnam, Sallie Ann Brock. *Richmond during the War: Four Years of Personal Observations by a Richmond Lady.* New York, 1867.

Pryor, Mrs. Roger A. *Reminiscences of Peace and War.* New York, 1924.

Ranson, John. *Andersonville Diary.* Middlebury, Vt., 1866.

Reagan, John H. *Memories with Special Reference to Secession and the Civil War.* New York, 1906.

Report of the Adjutant General of the State of Illinois. Vols. 1–7, 1861–1865. Springfield, Ohio, 1867.

Report of the Adjutant General of the State of New Hampshire for the Year Ending May 30, 1865. Vol. 1. Concord, 1865.

Ross, Isabel. *The President's Wife. Mary Todd Lincoln. A Biography.* New York, 1973.

Rudd, Alice Bohmer. *Shockoe Hill Cemetery, Richmond, Va., Register.* Richmond, 1960.

Ryan, David D. *Cornbread and Maggots, Cloak and Dagger: Union Soldiers and Spies in Civil War Richmond.* Richmond, 1994.

———. *Four Days in 1865: The Fall of Richmond.* Richmond, 1993.

———. *Richmond Illustrated: Unusual Stories of a City.* Richmond, 1993.

Sabre, G. E. *Nineteen Months a Prisoner of War.* New York, 1865.

Sandberg, Carl. *Abraham Lincoln: The War Years.* Vol. 2. New York, 1936.

Sanders, E. W., and C. W. Bowers. *Illustrated Richmond.* Richmond, 1908.

Small, Maj. A. R. *The Sixteenth Maine Regiment in the War of Rebellion, 1861–1865.* Portland, Maine, 1886.

Tennesseans in the Civil War. Vols. 1 & 2. Nashville, 1964.

Thayer, Pauline Revere. *A Memorial of Paul Joseph Revere and Edward H. R. Revere.* Clinton, Mass., 1874.

Thomas, Emory H. *The Confederates of Richmond. A Biography of the Capital.* Austin, Tex., 1991.

Townsend, William H. *Lincoln and the Bluegrass. Slavery and the Civil War in Kentucky.* Lexington, Ky., 1989.

Turner, Justin G., and Linda Levitt Turner. *Mary Todd Lincoln: Her Life and Letters.* New York, 1987.

Virginia: A Guide to the Old Dominion. New York, 1940.

Ward, Geoffrey C. *The Civil War.* New York, 1990.

War of Rebellion: A Compilation of the Official Records of the Union and Confederate Armies. Series I, Vols. 1–46 and Series II, Vols. 1–8. Washington, D.C., 1899.

ARTICLES

Anderson, D. R., ed. "Biographies of John Minor Botts, Richard Henry Lee, William Cabell Rives and John Moncure Daniel." "Richmond College Historical Papers," 1, no. 1 (June 1915).

Beaudry, Louis N. "The Libby Chronicle," 7 issues. Albany, N.Y. Privately printed, 1889.

Blakeless, John. "Lincoln's Private Spy." *Civil War Times Illustrated* (October 1975).

Bray, John. "Escape from Richmond." *Harper's Magazine* (April 1864).

Castel, Albert. "Samuel Ruth: Union Spy." *Civil War Times Illustrated* (February 1976).

"Confederate Inflation Chart," Official Publication No. 13, Richmond Civil War Centennial Commission (January 8, 1963).

Crossley, William J. "Memories." Rhode Island Soldiers and Sailors Historical Society, no. 4. Privately printed (1903).

Durham, Roger S. "The Biggest Yankee in the World." *Civil War Times Illustrated* (May 1974).

Flowers, Paul. "Too Brave to Die: The Sam Davis Spy Incident." *Civil War Times Illustrated* (August 1960).

Holzman, Dr. Robert S. "The Soldier with Two Sexes." *Civil War Times Illustrated* (January 1965).

"Libby Prison, Richmond, Virginia." Official Publication No. 12, Richmond Civil War Centennial Committee, Richmond (1961).

MacCauley, Lt. Clay. "From the Battlefield at Chancellorsville into

Libby Prison." Rhode Island Soldiers and Sailors Historical Society. Privately printed.

"Names of Soldiers Who Were Confined in Libby Prison during the Late War." Libby War Museum Association, Chicago (1889).

Parker, George C. "I feel . . . just like writing you a letter. . . ." *Civil War Times Illustrated* (April 1977).

Popcock, Barry. "The Adventures of Union Spy Pryce Lewis." *Civil War Times Illustrated* (September 1988).

Prey, Gilbert G. "Recollections of Rebel Prisons." *Historical Wyoming* (April 1865). Additional information courtesy of Robert B. Hoyt, Prey's grandson, Newark, Del.

Sampson, Captain Thomas. "Personal Narrative." Rhode Island Soldiers and Sailors Historical Society, privately printed (1883).

"The Prisoners at Richmond." *Harper's Weekly* (October 13, 1863).

"The Treatment of Prisoners during the War Between the States." *Southern Historical Society Papers,* 1, no. 3 (March 1876) and 1, no. 4 (April 1876).

Weitzel, Godfrey. "Richmond Occupied." Richmond Civil War Centennial Commission (1965).